STAR WARS™
THE CLONE WARS™

Beginning with a brief but significant mention in *Star Wars: A New Hope*, the Clone Wars were greatly expanded upon in the *Star Wars* prequel trilogy (1999-2005) before the animated *Star Wars: The Clone Wars* movie (2008) drew audiences into the heart of the galactic conflict that audiences had speculated about for 30 years.

The show went on to spawn seven seasons that explored the dramatic conflict as established characters such as Anakin Skywalker, Obi-Wan Kenobi, and Count Dooku were expanded upon, and new characters such as Captain Rex, Hondo Ohnaka, and, of course, Ahsoka Tano won the hearts and minds of audiences young and old.

Now, discover how this groundbreaking series was brought to life by a dedicated team, led by supervising director Dave Filoni and creator and executive producer George Lucas...

TITAN EDITORIAL
Editor Jonathan Wilkins
Group Editor Jake Devine
Art Director Oz Browne
Editorial Assistant Calum Collins
Production Controller Caterina Falqui
Production Controller Kelly Fenlon
Production Manager Jackie Flook
Sales and Circulation Manager Steve Tothill
Marketing Coordinator Lauren Noding
Acquisitions Editor Duncan Baizley
Publishing Director Ricky Claydon
Publishing Director John Dziewiatkowski
Operations Director Leigh Baulch
Publishers Nick Landau and Vivian Cheung

DISTRIBUTION
U.S. Newsstand: Total Publisher Services, Inc.
John Dziewiatkowski, 630-851-7683
U.S. Distribution: Ingrams Periodicals, Curtis Circulation Company
U.K. Newsstand: Marketforce, 0203 787 9199
U.S./U.K. Direct Sales Market: Diamond Comic Distributors

For more info on advertising contact adinfo@titanemail.com

First edition: January 2022

Star Wars: The Clone Wars The Official Collector's Edition is published by Titan Magazines, a division of Titan Publishing Group Limited, 144 Southwark Street, London, SE1 0UP

Printed in the U.S.A.
For sale in the U.S., UK, and Canada

ISBN: 9781787737167
Titan Authorized User.
TMN 14165

A CIP catalogue record for this title is available from the British Library.

10 9 8 7 6 5 4 3 2 1

DISNEY PUBLISHING WORLDWIDE GLOBAL MAGAZINES, COMICS, AND PARTWORKS
Publisher: Lynn Waggoner
Editorial Director: Bianca Coletti
Editorial Team: Guido Frazzini (Director, Comics),Stefano Ambrosio (Executive Editor, New IP),Carlotta Quattrocolo (Executive Editor,Franchise), Camilla Vedove (Senior Manager,Editorial Development), Behnoosh Khalili (Senior Editor), Julie Dorris (Senior Editor),Mina Riazi (Assistant Editor), Gabriella Capasso (Assistant Editor))
Design: Enrico Soave (Senior Designer)
Art: Ken Shue (VP, Global Art), Roberto Santillo (Creative Director), Marco Ghiglione (Creative Manager), Manny Mederos (Creative Manager), Stefano Attardi (Illustration Manager)
Portfolio Management: Olivia Ciancarelli (Director)

Business & Marketing: Mariantonietta Galla (Senior Manager, Franchise), Virpi Korhonen (Editorial Manager)
Text: W. Rathbone, Landry Walker
Graphic Design: Falcinelli & Co. / Mauro Abbattista Pre-Press: Lito milano srl

LUCASFILM
Senior Editor: Brett Rector
Creative Director of Publishing: Michael Siglain
Art Director: Troy Alders
Story Group: Pablo Hidalgo, Leland Chee
Creative Art Manager: Phil Szostak
Asset Management: Chris Argyropoulos, Gabrielle Levenson, Shahana Alam
Thanks to: Tracy Cannobbio

CONTENTS

THE CLONE WARS

Across hundreds of planets, Republic forces battle against the Separatists for the future of the galaxy. The Republic army's genetically engineered clone troopers are led by the Jedi Order—together, they fight to restore peace to the galaxy. Against them are the never-ending droid army commanded by the sinister Count Dooku, who answers to a mysterious Sith Lord known only as Darth Sidious...

It all began when Obi-Wan Kenobi found out that a secret clone army had been ordered by Jedi Master Sifo-Dyas from alien cloners on the planet Kamino. During his investigation, he discovered a secret droid army was being made by the Geonosians in their factories—paid for by the Separatists. Soon after, Obi-Wan, Anakin Skywalker, and Padmé Amidala were captured and under threat of execution, leading the Jedi and clone troopers to attack the droid army at the First Battle of Geonosis, which marked the beginning of the Clone Wars.

THE MOVIE

Set in the events between the movies *Attack of the Clones* (2002) and *Revenge of the Sith* (2005), *Star Wars: The Clone Wars* (2008) was released as a feature film in theaters across the world, introducing *Star Wars* to a new generation of fans. It also opened the way to the TV series, bringing to the screen key characters and the struggle between the Sith and the Jedi.

George Lucas saw this animated approach as a chance to revisit the concept of the Clone Wars, being previously mentioned in the live-action films, and he drew from anime and manga as inspiration in the process.

Set after the First Battle of Geonosis, we open with the Outer Rim in peril, and the Republic facing an imminent defeat. The only hope the forces of the Jedi have is to secure safe passage for their ships through systems controlled by the Hutt Syndicate. And at last, an opportunity has a risen – the child of the gangster Jabba the Hutt has been kidnapped, and the Jedi are the only ones who might rescue him. Obi-Wan Kenobi and his former pupil Anakin Skywalker are given the task, and are joined by a young Padawan named Ahsoka Tano, assigned to Anakin for training. Though inexperienced, Ahsoka brings an unmatched enthusiasm for victory to the battlefield, and puts Anakin's patience to the test. The search for Jabba's son leads Anakin and Ahsoka to the planet Teth, where they are ambushed by a battalion of droids led by the dark-side assassin, Assaj Ventress – now apprentice to Count Dooku. During this battle they learn the truth – Dooku is using the Jedi, setting them up to appear as the real kidnappers. The goal, to incite a feud between the criminal underground and the Jedi Council.

Learning that Anakin is in trouble with the Hutt's, Senator Padmé Amidala embarks upon her own investigation – discovering that Jabba's scheming uncle Ziro the Hutt is in alliance with Count Dooku, and is responsible for the kidnapping. Though the Jedi are saved by Padmé's intervention, Darth Sidious is pleased. The Republic will believe they have won a great victory - but the Sith are planning to win an entire war... ☰

WHO FOUGHT IN THE CLONE WARS

Millions of clone troopers and battle droids fought on hundreds of planets throughout the galactic conflict known as the Clone Wars. Though thousands of nameless soldiers perished, the commanders and Jedi generals who lead them into battle will live on forever.

ANAKIN SKYWALKER

Discovered as a slave on Tatooine by Jedi Master Qui-Gon Jinn, Anakin Skywalker had the potential to become one of the most powerful Jedi ever. His midi-chlorian count was off the charts—which lead Qui-Gon to believe that Anakin is the prophesied Chosen One, the being who would bring balance to the Force. A hero of the Clone Wars, Anakin is caring and compassionate, but also has a reputation amongst the Jedi for passion, recklessness, and overconfidence.

1 / When Anakin voice actor Matt Lanter went in for his audition for *The Clone Wars*, he was told by his agent he was auditioning for a character called "Deak Starkiller."

2 / During The *Clone Wars*, audiences see flashes of the dark side surfacing within Anakin Skywalker. The young Jedi serves as the connective tissue between *Attack of the Clones* (2002) and *Revenge of the Sith* (2005).

Anakin Skywalker was voiced by Matt Lanter, who has acted in shows, films, and video games, including *Ultimate Spider-Man*, LEGO *Star Wars: The Force Awakens*, and the TV series *90210*.

1 /

3 / The design for Ob-Wan Kenobi was partially inspired by the 2D Genndy Tartakovsky *Clone Wars* micro-series, with elements of his traditional Jedi tunic combined with clone trooper armor.

3 /

OBI-WAN KENOBI

A legendary Jedi Master, Obi-Wan Kenobi was a noble and free-thinking Jedi, gifted in the ways of the Force. He studied as a Padawan under Jedi Master Qui-Gon Jinn. After Qui-Gon was killed by the Sith Lord Darth Maul, Obi-Wan ascended to the role of Jedi Knight and trained Anakin Skywalker. They both served the Republic together as generals during the Clone Wars. Later, Obi-Wan would mentor and guide Luke Skywalker.

Obi-Wan Kenobi was voiced by James Arnold Taylor, whose prolific career includes shows, films, and video games, such as LEGO *City Adventure* and the TV series *Guardians of the Galaxy* and *Scooby-Doo! Mystery Incorporated*.

4 /

AHSOKA TANO

Ahsoka Tano, a Togruta from the planet Shili, was Padawan to Anakin Skywalker, and who also became a hero of the Clone Wars. Alongside Anakin, she grew from a headstrong student into a mature leader. But her destiny would lay on a different path from that of the Jedi Order.

Ahsoka Tano was voiced by Ashley Eckstein, whose voice can be heard in many shows, video games, and films, including *Star Wars Rebels*, *Star Wars Forces of Destiny*, LEGO *Star Wars III: The Clone Wars*, and *The Rise of Skywalker*, as well as TV series *Sofia the First* and *That's So Raven*. Eckstein also founded a fashion house called Her Universe.

4 / When the show was first conceived, Ahsoka's name was "Ashla," apprentice to a Twi'lek Jedi named Sendlak.

CLONE CAPTAIN REX

Spawned in the clone factories of Kamino, Captain Rex (CC-7567) served the Republic during the Clone Wars, often under the command of Anakin Skywalker and Ahsoka Tano. He viewed military service as an honor, and does his best to take care of his fellow clone troopers.

Fond of using two blaster pistols at the same time, Rex customizes his armor with distinctive blue markings. However, even this dedicated clone is plagued by doubts as the Clone Wars claim more lives and bring terrible destruction to more worlds.

Captain Rex (and all the clone troopers) was voiced by Dee Bradley Baker, whose credits include *Phineas and Ferb*, *Space Jam*, and the TV series *American Dad!*

YODA

Yoda is perhaps the most legendary and respected Jedi Master. It is said that his connection with the Force is stronger than any other Jedi's. Though small in size, Yoda has trained Jedi apprentices for over 800 years. A member of the Jedi Council, he plays an integral role in the Clone Wars, the instruction of Luke Skywalker, and unlocking the path to a kind of immortality.

Yoda was voiced by Tom Kane (who also performs the opening narration for each episode), who has also provided voices for characters in projects including *Prince Valiant*, *Shrek 3*, and the TV series *The Avengers*.

5 /

5 / Yoda's design exaggerates the Jedi Master's features - his hands, feet, and eyes are all much larger than they are in the films - so that they can be more expressive on the small screen.

MACE WINDU

A determined Jedi Master with an amethyst-bladed lightsaber, Mace Windu is also a member of the Jedi Council. As such he has little tolerance for the failings of the Senate, the arguments of politicians, or the opinions of rebellious Jedi. As the Clone Wars intensify, Mace senses the dark side of the Force at work, and know the Jedi's enemies are plotting to destroy the Jedi Order and plunge the galaxy into chaos.

Mace Windu was voiced by Terrence "T.C." Carson, an actor familiar to fans films, video games, and TV shows such as *Life with Louie*, *Living Single*, and *Clifford the Big Red Dog*.

SUPREME CHANCELLOR PALPATINE/ DARTH SIDIOUS

The dark side of the Force is a pathway to many abilities some consider to be unnatural, and Supreme Chancellor Palpatine is the most infamous follower of these Sith doctrines as his alter ego Darth Sidious. Scheming, powerful, and greedy, Darth Sidious wishes to elevate the Sith and destroy the Jedi Order. Living a double life, Sidious plays the role of Supreme Chancellor Palpatine in public, the phantom menace who is slowly but surely manipulating the political system of the Galactic Republic to his own nefarious ends

Palpatine/Sidious was voiced by Ian Abercrombie, a veteran of stage and films, as well as video games, *Army of Darkness*, and TV shows *Santa Barbara* and *Fantasy Island*.

PADMÉ AMIDALA

Padmé Amidala served as Queen of Naboo and when her term was completed, she became a Senator of Naboo. Not only a politician, she is also handy with a blaster, fighting in the field on behalf of the Republic. Despite her commitment to political honesty, she is secretly married to the Jedi Anakin Skywalker, and the two will occasionally share an adventure.

Padmé Amidala was voiced by Catherine Taber, whose credits also include films, video games, and TV shows such as *The Loud House*, *Jane the Virgin*, and *Robot Chicken*.

COUNT DOOKU

Sith Lord Count Dooku is a central figure in the Clone Wars. Once a Jedi and former apprentice of Yoda, he became disillusioned with the Jedi Order and thirsted for greater power. Dooku voluntarily left the light side behind to become Darth Sidious' secret disciple, taking the name Darth Tyranus. As Count Dooku, he leads the Separatist army and battles the Jedi generals.

Count Dooku was voiced by Corey Burton, a veteran of many films as well as the video game *Atlantis: The Lost Empire*, and TV shows *DuckTales* and *Future-Worm*!

GENERAL GRIEVOUS

6 / General Grevious is
a member of the race
called the Kaleesh.
Though his mask
evokes the culture of
his people, there is
very little Kaleesh left
of the cyborg.

6 / The design of
Grevious was meant to
foreshadow Anakin's
own cybernetic fate.

More machine than flesh, General Grievous is a diabolical
Separatist military strategist and a feared Jedi hunter, known
for his ruthlessness and hacking cough. His body itself is a
weapon, enabling the cyborg to make lightning strikes and
devastating blows.

General Grievous is voiced by Matthew Wood, who also
voices the show's many battle and commando droids, as
well as Wat Tambor, Poggle the Lesser, Amani, Derrown
and other character. If that's enough he is also *The Clone
Wars'* supervising sound editor. He originally won the role of
Grievous for *Revenge of the Sith*.

7 /

C-3PO

C-3PO knows more than six million forms of communication, something that keeps the worry-prone droid on the frontlines of the galactic conflict. Originally built by young Anakin Skywalker to help his mother, Shmi, he eventually became a protocol droid for the Rebel Alliance and then the Republic. C-3PO is a frequent companion of the astromech droid R2-D2.

C-3PO is voiced by Anthony Daniels, who originated the character for the very first *Star Wars* movie in 1977. Daniels is the only actor to appear in all nine of the *Star Wars* episodic movies. In *Attack of the Clones* he had a cameo as Dannl Faytoni, allowing fans for the first time to see Daniels in a *Star Wars* film without his droid costume.

R2-D2

The ever-reliable and versatile astromech droid R2-D2 tirelessly serves the side of good in the Clone Wars. Over many years, R2-D2 serves Padmé Amidala, Anakin Skywalker, and, eventually, Luke Skywalker, showing great bravery in rescuing his masters and their friends from many perils. A skilled starship mechanic and fighter pilot's assistant, he has an unlikely but enduring friendship with the fussy protocol droid, C-3PO.

R2-D2 is "voiced" by *The Clone Wars* series' sound department. His original bleeps, beeps, and coos were created by sound designer Ben Burtt for the first six *Star Wars* movies.

JAR JAR BINKS

A clumsy but well-meaning Gungan, Jar Jar Binks leaves his underwater homeworld of Naboo to enter the murkier waters of Coruscant politics. As a representative for his people in the Galactic Capital, Jar Jar embarks on many missions and ends up in quite a few dangerous, but comic situations, despite his best intentions.

Jar Jar Binks is voiced by Ahmed Best, who played Binks in the *Star Wars* prequel trilogy. Best is a veteran of, among other films, shorts, and video games, the TV series *Easy To Assemble* and *Big Time Rush*.

SEASON 1
EPISODE GUIDE

EP. 1 "AMBUSH"

Yoda voyages to the coral moon of Rugosa to convince Toydaria's King Katuunko to help the Republic, but Asajj Ventress also seeks the king's allegiance. After Yoda's ship is shot down, he proposes a wager: He and his small squad of clone troopers will battle Ventress's massive droid army. The winner will obtain Katuunko's aid.

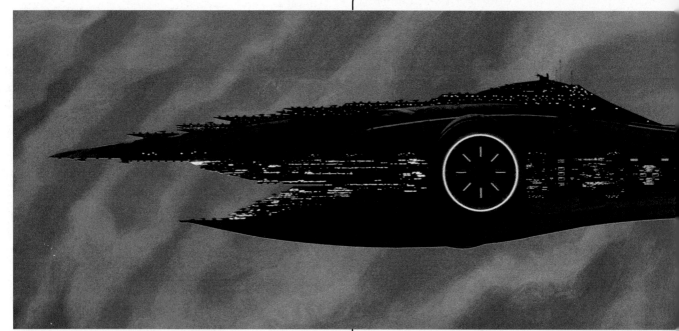

EP. 2 "RISING MALEVOLENCE"

EP. 3 "SHADOW OF MALEVOLENCE"

EP. 4 "DESTROY MALEVOLENCE"

A devastating new Separatist ion-cannon weapon aboard the powerful starship *Malevolence*, commanded by General Grievous, maroons Jedi Master Plo Koon and two clone troopers, led by clone commander Wolffe. Disobeying the Jedi Council, Anakin Skywalker and Ahsoka Tano search for them.

After finding their comrades, the Separatists attack Republic medical facilities, so Anakin utilizes new long-range Y-wing bombers to lead a bold strike on the *Malevolence*, with the help of Ahsoka, Plo, and Plo's clone troopers.

Anakin damages the *Malevolence*. However, Senator Padmé Amidala (Anakin's wife) and C-3PO are taken hostage by Grievous, which means Anakin and Obi-Wan have to save them, too, before they can destroy the enemy ship — but Grievous awaits…

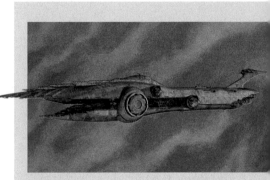

DATA & TRIVIA

- A gargantuan heavy cruiser, the *Malevolence* is known for its immense ion-cannons, which are a strategic threat to the Republic fleet early in the Clone Wars. The cruiser's deadly two-step attack: knock out the power systems of an enemy vessel with its primary weapon; finish them off with blasts from its secondary laser cannons and turbolaser batteries.

- Voice actor Tom Kane provides the voice of **Yoda**, and narrates the opening of each episode of *The Clone Wars*.

EP. 5 "ROOKIES"

Commanders Rex and Cody arrive at a distant outpost on the Rishi Moon for a routine inspection. When they are surprised by a droid commando raid, the officers must inspire their rookie unit to believe in themselves and defeat their adversaries.

EP. 6 "DOWNFALL OF A DROID"

EP. 7 "DUEL OF THE DROIDS"

R2-D2 disappears during a fierce space battle, and Anakin Skywalker must find him before the Separatists discover the military secrets locked in the droid's memory banks. Anakin, Ahsoka Tano, and their replacement droid, R3-S6, embark on a rescue and sabotage mission when they discover R2 is being held at General Grievous's secret listening post, Skytop Station.

EP. 8 "BOMBAD JEDI"

EP. 9 "CLOAK OF DARKNESS"

EP. 10 "LAIR OF GRIEVOUS"

On a diplomatic mission to the planet Rodia, Padmé Amidala discovers that her old friend and fellow senator Onaconda Farr has allied his planet with the Separatists. He betrays her to an old nemesis, Nute Gunray. Sensing Padmé is in trouble, Gungan Jar Jar Binks disguises himself as a Jedi—can he rescue Padmé?

Ahsoka and Jedi Master Luminara Unduli capture Gunray and escort him to Coruscant, where he can stand trial for his crimes. Under orders from Count Dooku, Asajj Ventress attempts to free Gunray; the Jedi fight back with the help of Senate Commandos, but Gunray escapes.

Jedi Master Kit Fisto and his former Padawan, Mon Calamari Jedi Nahdar Vebb, track Gunray to a remote moon, where they enter a mysterious den filled with strange creatures and weapons—the deadly lair of General Grievous.

DATA & TRIVIA

- **Ahsoka Tano** has pet names for many of her friends, such as "Skyguy" for Anakin Skywalker and "Rexter" for Captain Rex.

- In "Downfall of a Droid" and "Duel of the Droids," **R3-S6's black-and-gold color scheme** recalls the colors of supervising director Dave Filoni's hometown football team, the Pittsburgh Steelers.

- The **Kwazel Maw design** in "Bombad Jedi" was based on legendary artist Ralph McQuarrie's concept for a swamp slug creature (it would have dwelled on the planet Dagobah in *The Empire Strikes Back*).

EP. 11 "DOOKU CAPTURED"

EP. 12 "THE GUNGAN GENERAL"

While trying to capture Count Dooku, Anakin Skywalker and Obi-Wan Kenobi find the Sith Lord has already been captured by pirates, led by Hondo Ohnaka, who are holding him for ransom on Florrum. The Jedi are also captured. The Republic sends the ransom via a special shuttle commanded by Representative Jar Jar Binks, and a battle erupts. Oddly, the Jedi find themselves united with Dooku in order to win their freedom.

- **Lok Durd** is voiced by veteran actor George Takei, who played Sulu on the original *Star Trek* series.

EP. 13 "JEDI CRASH"

EP. 14 "DEFENDERS OF PEACE"

Anakin Skywalker and Ahsoka Tano are assisting Jedi General Aayla Secura during an atmospheric battle when Anakin is injured. The Jedi, Captain Rex, and the surviving clones crashland on Maridun and make their way to a Lurmen village. Their ruler, Tee Watt Kaa, explains that the Lurmen are pacifists, but they agree to help save Anakin's life.

Separatist weapons expert General Lok Durd arrives to test a devastating weapon, which they plan to use on the Lurmen! The villagers have to decide whether to sacrifice themselves or fight with the Jedi to defend their village.

EP. 15 "TRESPASS"

On the desolate ice world Orto Plutonia, Anakin Skywalker and Obi-Wan Kenobi investigate the disappearance of a clone security force, only to discover a tribe of furry natives known as the Talz, fierce beast-riding warriors. Can they make peace with them?

EP. 16 "THE HIDDEN ENEMY"

Anakin Skywalker and Obi-Wan Kenobi lead Republic forces against droid armies to free the planet of Christophsis from a Separatist siege—but are ambushed and forced to retreat. Is there a traitor among them? And if he is a clone, how can Commander Cody and Captain Rex outthink an enemy who is just like them?

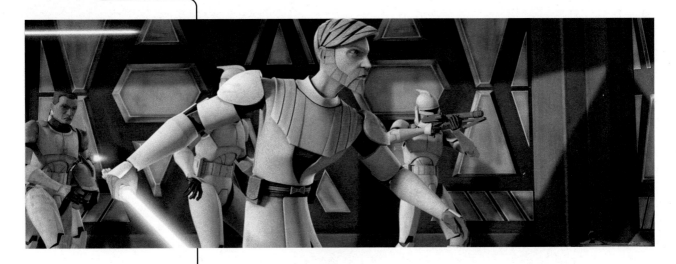

EP. 17 "BLUE SHADOW VIRUS"

EP. 18 "MYSTERY OF A THOUSAND MOONS"

Padmé Amidala discovers a Separatist bio-weapon lab hidden on Naboo and is taken prisoner by its sinister scientist Dr. Nuvo Vindi, who threatens to release the lethal Blue Shadow virus! Anakin Skywalker and Obi-Wan Kenobi travel to the mysterious planet, Iego, to secure the antidote—but must solve a mystery before they can leave…

DATA & TRIVIA

- Anakin Skywalker and **General Grievous** meet for the first time in the movie *Star Wars*: Episode III *Revenge of the Sith*. In *The Clone Wars* series, which takes place before the movie, their armies fight each other, but the two never actually meet.

- In *The Phantom Menace* a young Anakin Skywalker asks Padmé Amidala, "Are you an **angel?**" During the Clone Wars years later, Skywalker travels to the Moons of Iego in "Mystery of a Thousand Moons," where angels are said to dwell.

Ryloth, homeworld of the Twi'lek, is blockaded by Trade Federation battleships. While launching a surprise attack, Ahsoka Tano disobeys Anakin Skywalker and loses most of her squadron. Anakin helps Ahsoka to regain faith in herself, placing her in charge of another risky attack, and she helps destroy the blockade. Obi-Wan Kenobi then leads a small clone force into a droid-occupied town to sabotage their anti-aircraft guns. When another droid army, led by Wat Tambor, attacks, Jedi Mace Windu must convince Twi'lek freedom fighter Cham Syndulla to help him save the planet.

DATA & TRIVIA

- **Ryloth** is the principal planet in the Ryloth system located in the Outer Rim near Tatooine. It is home to the Twi'leks, a humanoid species with two large, fleshy head-tails growing from their skulls, "lekku." During the Clone Wars, scheming Separatist warlords blockade and invade Ryloth, hoping to steal its riches.

EP. 22 "HOSTAGE CRISIS"

In order to force the release of crime lord Ziro the Hutt from prison, bounty hunters seize control of the Senate Building and hold members of the Senate hostage. Bounty hunter Cad Bane, with the help of Aurra Sing, issues his demands to to Supreme Chancellor Palpatine. Unbeknownst to the bad guys, Anakin Skywalker is loose in the Senate...

DATA & TRIVIA

- "Hostage Crisis" actually fits into a story arc that takes place in Season 3!

FAMOUS BATTLES

1. The Republic fleet approaches Ryloth, as troops on the ground attack in coordinated strikes against the Separatists.

2. On the attack, a droid squadron unleashes a barrage of blaster fire against their clone enemies.

3. Anakin Skywalker and Obi-Wan Kenobi battle their way through the *Malevolence*. And though violence is not the Jedi way, the lightsaber is a powerful tool against the droid army.

4. The destructive defoliator deployment tank, or DDT, is a modified vehicle that launches biological warheads capable of destroying organic life without damaging machines or buildings.

5. Obi-Wan Kenobi and Anakin Skywalker search the planet Christophsis for a traitor, and they are surprised by an ambush from a familiar foe.

4.

5.

SEASON 2
EPISODE GUIDE

EP. 1 "HOLOCRON HEIST"

EP. 2 "CARGO OF DOOM"

EP. 3 "CHILDREN OF THE FORCE"

Cad Bane is hired by Darth Sidious to steal a powerful Jedi holocron. The holocrons – data storage systems that can be opened only with the Force – are protected within a vault inside the Jedi Temple. Bane recruits a changeling named Cato Parasitti, who poses as Madame Jocasta Nu, the librarian inside the Jedi Archive, to infiltrate the building's security systems. Ahsoka Tano catches on, she, Anakin Skywalker and Obi-Wan Kenobi give chase to Bane and his cohorts.

Anakin and Ahsoka travel to the planet Devaron in pursuit of Bane. But Bane has trapped Jedi Bolla Ropal, keeper of the kyber memory crystal, which will reveal data on every known Force-sensitive child in the galaxy when combined with the holocron. But, after failing with Ropal, Bane captures Ahsoka, and forces Anakin to open the holocron to save his Padawan.

Darth Sidious hires Bane to kidnap several Force-sensitive children to train as dark-side spies. Bane does his job until he is captured on Naboo by Anakin and Ahsoka, and brought before Obi-Wan and Mace Windu to have his mind probed. Unable to resist their Force powers, Bane agrees to lead Kenobi and Windu to his hidden base and the holocron, while Anakin and Ahsoka venture to Mustafar to save the stolen children from Sidious' evil plot.

DATA & TRIVIA

- Cad Bane's techno-service droid has many built in gadgets that make him useful, but he also has an abrasive attitude. **Todo 360** is a hard worker and reminds others of this fact—often.

- Todo 360, Bane's droid, is voiced by Seth Green, who co-created and co-executive produced the stop-motion sketch comedy television series, *Robot Chicken*.

The Jedi Council suspects that Senator Rush Clovis, an InterGalactic Banking Clan delegate and former colleague of Padmé Amidala, may be working for the Separatists. Against Anakin Skywalker's wishes, the Council asks Padmé if she would accompany Rush to Cato Neimoidia to check on the senator's allegiances. Fending off Anakin's jealousy, as well as an attempt on her life by Neimoidian Lott Dod, Padmé does her duty and discovers that the Geonosians are secretly building droids.

DATA & TRIVIA

- Designers added personality to the gunships in "Landing at Point Rain," including an illustration of a nexu with the phrase "Bad Kitty" scrawled beneath it, an homage to the Industrial Light & Magic animation crew who had nicknamed the creature during the making of *Attack of the Clones*.

Anakin Skywalker, Obi-Wan Kenobi, and Ki-Adi-Mundi lead an invasion to stop Poggle the Lesser and the Geonosians from rebuilding their droid army. Things go wrong, however, when Geonosian forces shoot down the Republic ships, which crash land. Under increasing pressure, Anakin, Obi-Wan, and Ki-Adi-Mundi have their own set of challenges to overcome -- hordes of enemy troops, deadly traps, unforgiving terrain, and a massive energy shield.

Anakin, Ahsoka, Jedi Master Luminara Unduli and her Padawan, Barriss Offee, lead a mission to destroy the droid factory. But Poggle the Lesser deploys his newest weapon, indestructible super tanks. The Jedi

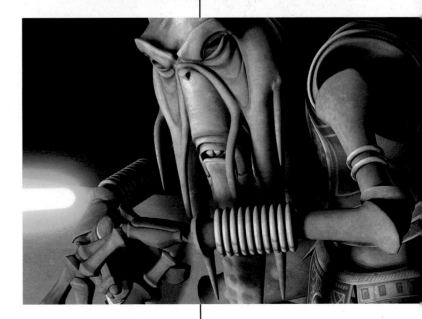

devise a daring plan in which Anakin and Luminara act as decoys to divert the super tanks, while Ahsoka and Barriss infiltrate the plant via a labyrinth of catacombs beneath the city.

After a battle to destroy a new droid factory on Geonosis, Master Unduli disappears while tracking Poggle the Lesser. Obi-Wan and Anakin lead a platoon of clone troopers in search of her and descend deep into the subterranean temple of Karina the Great, the Geonosian Queen. To their horror, they learn that the hive is alive and teeming with undead defenders. The queen can reanimate and control her subjects.

While the Jedi Knights transport Poggle the Lesser as a prisoner to Coruscant, Padawans Barriss and Ahsoka are dispatched to escort a medical frigate to its destination. When Geonosian brain worms take control of the clone troopers aboard their supply ship, Ahsoka and Barriss must battle to stop the vessel from unleashing the deadly plague upon the galaxy.

EP. 9 **"GRIEVOUS INTRIGUE"**

EP. 10 **"THE DESERTER"**

Jedi Master Eeth Koth is taken hostage and tortured by General Grievous. Anakin Skywalker, Obi-Wan Kenobi and Adi Gallia devise a daring rescue plan, but soon realize the general has a plan of his own. The Jedi and the Separatist general try to outmaneuver each other in a ship-to-ship and hand-to-hand battle high over the planet Saleucami.

Grievous is shot down over Saleucami and crash lands in the wilderness. Obi-Wan leads an expedition to find the droid general. Captain Rex is injured during the search, and must recover in a local barn that he is shocked to discover is owned by a farmer named Cut Lawquane, a clone deserter who has a family.

DATA & TRIVIA

- Covered by a single immense cityscape, **Coruscant** is capital of the galaxy. It features towering buildings, streams of speeder-filled air traffic, and mysterious levels that descend far below the city's surface. Coruscant is the seat of government for the Galactic Republic. It is also home to the Jedi Temple and the Jedi Order.

- The MagnaGuards' electrostaffs in "Grievous Intrigue" are made of phrik, an alloy that resists the blades of lightsabers.

- In "Lightsaber Lost," Chief Librarian of the Jedi Archives Jocasta Nu and Ahsoka Tano, while doing research, come across the familiar face of Brea Tonnika, one of the Tonnika sisters glimpsed in the cantina at Mos Eisley in *A New Hope*.

EP. 11 **"LIGHTSABER LOST"**

During an assignment in the Coruscant underworld, a wily pickpocket steals Ahsoka Tano's lightsaber. Ahsoka enlists the help of an elderly Jedi, Tera Sinube, to track down her weapon and learn the art of patience.

EP. 12 "THE MANDALORE PLOT"

EP. 13 "VOYAGE OF TEMPTATION"

EP. 14 "DUCHESS OF MANDALORE"

Alarming reports about attacks on the peace-abiding Duchess Satine Kryze of Mandalore prompt Obi-Wan Kenobi to visit the secluded planet. Satine wants to keep Mandalore neutral in the Clone Wars, but the actions of a violent splinter group – Death Watch – threaten to push the planet towards global war.

Duchess Satine travels from Mandalore to Coruscant on a diplomatic mission, with Obi-Wan, Anakin Skywalker and a team of troopers to defend her. As her luxurious starship, *Coronet*, makes its way through hyperspace, the Jedi must stop several assassination attempts, and Anakin discovers that Obi-Wan and the duchess have a romantic history together.

On Coruscant, word reaches Duchess Satine that Death Watch plans to spark a pre-emptive Republic invasion. On the run, Satine and Obi-Wan set off to discover the group's true motives and prevent the bloody conflict. This arc introduces the Darksaber - a unique black bladed-lightsaber that serves as a symbol of leadership. This artifact goes on to be a part of *The Mandalorian* live-action series, eventually being won in battle by Din Djarin.

EP. 15 "SENATE MURDERS"

Padmé Amidala argues against outrageous military spending, but her mentor, Senator Onaconda Farr, dies under suspicious circumstances. She sets out to find the person who poisoned him, entering a dangerous world of backstabbing, lies, and secrets controlled by the powerful senators Mee Deechi and Halle Burtoni.

EP. 16 "CAT AND MOUSE"

A Separatist blockade prevents the planet Christophsis from getting much-needed relief supplies. Anakin Skywalker's fleet is tasked with deploying supplies to the surface, but they are massively out-gunned and out-maneuvered by the skillful Admiral Trench. Obi-Wan Kenobi arrives and unveils the Republic's new weapon: a stealth ship, their last hope at defeating Trench and aiding the battered people of Christophsis.

EP. 17 "BOUNTY HUNTERS"

Anakin, Obi-Wan, and Ahsoka crash land on Felucia and seek aid from the local spice farmers only to learn that the farmers are the ones who are in real need. Beset by Hondo Ohnaka and his band of pirates, who plan to steal their crops, the farmers have contracted four lethal bounty hunters to protect their wares. In an unlikely partnership, the Jedi must work with the farmers' hired guns to beat back Hondo and his brigands.

DATA & TRIVIA

- **Felucia** is a world teeming with fungal life-forms and immense primitive plants. Much of the planet has a fetid, humid landscape overgrown by forests of bizarre wilderness. Many of the life-forms on Felucia are partially or completely translucent; they color the sunlight as the beams penetrate their skin.

- Although it originally aired during the second season, "Cat and Mouse" is the first episode in *The Clone Wars* series, when viewed in chronological story order.

- In "Cat and Mouse," **Admiral Trench** resembles a large spider, hence his original name: Taranch (short for tarantula).

- The character Embo in "Bounty Hunters" has at least two things in common with Dave Filoni: The supervising director provides the voice of the alien and they both favor eccentric hats. This episode is also an homage to Kurosawa's movie, *Seven Samurai* (1954).

EP. 18 **"THE ZILLO BEAST"**

EP. 19 **"THE ZILLO BEAST STRIKES BACK"**

Desperate to turn the tide of a fierce battle on Malastare and win a strategic alliance with the Dugs, Supreme Chancellor Palpatine orders the Jedi to drop the Republic's newest superweapon, an untested electro-proton bomb. The bomb's blast awakens an ancient and fearsome Zillo Beast, a monster of legendary size and ferocity. Now the Jedi must contain this deadly creature despite the interference of the bloodthirsty Dugs, who wish to kill the beast. But Mace Windu succeeds in capturing it.

Following Palpatine's orders, Republic forces transport the Zillo Beast back to Coruscant for scientific study and military gain. Palpatine plans to have the monster killed, but the Zillo Beast escapes from the lab and begins devastating the city. Anakin Skywalker, Padmé Amidala, and Palpatine are pursued by the beast while the Jedi fight to contain it at the Senate building. In a climactic showdown, the Jedi are faced with having to save the lives of millions of people on Coruscant by destroying the Zillo Beast, the last of its kind.

EP. 20 "DEATH TRAP"

EP. 21 *"ARTOO COME HOME"*

EP. 22 **"LETHAL TRACKDOWN"**

Young Boba Fett is determined to avenge the death of his father, Jango Fett, who was killed in battle by Jedi Master Mace Windu. He poses as a clone cadet and sneaks aboard a Jedi cruiser, the *Endurance*, to plant a bomb in Windu's quarters. The blast fails to kill the Jedi and, suddenly, every clone aboard is looking for the saboteur. Fett destroys the ship's reactor to create a distraction and the entire cruiser begins to break apart. Unaware that Boba is the culprit, his cadet comrades save his life.

Boba and his band of bounty hunters then lead Anakin Skywalker and Mace into a trap on Vanqor. It's up to R2-D2 to journey back to Coruscant and warn the Jedi of their comrades' desperate situation. Battling beast and bounty hunter along the way, the trusty droid finally communicates his warning to Ahsoka Tano and Plo Koon, who rush to Vanqor to save Mace and Anakin from a fiery death.

Fett and Aurra Sing go into hiding. Plo Koon and Ahsoka search the lower depths of Coruscant and the underworld, and learn that Fett, Sing, and bounty hunter Bossk are hiding out on Florrum.

In a showdown, Sing abandons Fett, who is taken prisoner by the Republic. He vows revenge once more…

DATA & TRIVIA

- Boba Fett was one of the most feared bounty hunters in the galaxy. A genetic clone of his "father," bounty hunter Jango Fett, Boba learned combat and martial skills from a young age. Over the course of his career, which included contracts for the Empire and the criminal underworld, he became a legend.

- When the *Endurance* suffers a hull breach, one of the troopers caught in the blast lets out a "Wilhelm scream," a sound effect that dates back to the 1930s. Sound designer Ben Burtt has used it in every *Star Wars* film up to 2005.

FAMOUS BATTLES

1. Anakin Skywalker fights against impossible odds on Geonosis, and the only thing that might save him is Ahsoka Tano's willingness to sacrifice herself for her master, and the mission.

2. When Geonosian brain worms attack, who can be trusted becomes impossible to know...

3. General Grevious escalate the war, believing that it his his responsibility to cleanse the galaxy of Jedi "filth."

4. The nature of the Zillo Beast is a mystery... is it a monster, or just an animal whose life the war has disrupted?

5. Boba Fett trades on his appearance as a clone to strike against the troopers that stand in his way – but balks at killing.

6. Aurra Sing holds innocent lives at her mercy, and only the pirate Hondo Ohnaka can convince Boba Fett to tell the Jedi where they are held.

DATA & TRIVIA

- The DC-15A is a powerful blaster, often used by clone troopers.

- The rain-swept world of **Kamino** was secretly deleted from the star maps in the Jedi Archives—until Obi-Wan Kenobi located it. A lonely world beyond the Outer Rim just south of the Rishi Maze, Kamino is an ocean planet; cities on enormous stilts tower over the waves. In Tipoca City, Prime Minister Lama Su closely monitors the business of Kamino's most prized export: clone troopers.

- The leader of Mandalore during the Clone Wars, **duchess Satine Kryze** of Kalevala pushes her people to move beyond its violent past and institute a government that values peace. Mandalore begins to rebuild under her guidance, but the dark shadow of the Clone Wars make the duchess' goals difficult to achieve.

- In "Supply Lines" the Jedi's name Ima-Gun Di is an obvious hint as to his ultimate fate: "I'm a-gonna die."

- In "Sphere of Influence," the Papanoida family is based on George Lucas and his children: Katie, Amanda, and Jett.

EP. 1 "CLONE CADETS"

Five selfish clones struggle to complete their training on Kamino. These cadets, known as "Domino Squad" – Hevy, Cutup, Droidbait, Fives, and Echo – seem to be failures and are unable to work as a team. Jedi Master Shaak Ti and drill instructors Bric and El-Les debate the cadets' dubious fate…

EP. 2 "ARC TROOPERS"

The Republic learns of an impending Separatist attack on Kamino; Anakin Skywalker and Obi-Wan Kenobi hurry to the planet. General Grievous and an army of droids rise out of the ocean, bent on destroying the clone production facilities, while Ventress infiltrates the lab on a secret mission. Captain Rex, Commander Cody, Fives and Echo lead the clones in a desperate defense of their home planet.

EP. 3 "SUPPLY LINES"

The Twi'lek planet of Ryloth is under siege. Trapped on the surface, Jedi Master Ima-Gun Di rallies local forces with the help of Cham Syndulla, but supplies are running out.

EP. 4 "SPHERE OF INFLUENCE"

The Trade Federation has blockaded Pantora to bully Chairman Baron Papanoida into joining the Separatists. His daughters, Chi Eekway and Che Amanwe Papnoida, are kidnapped and held for ransom. Ahsoka Tano teams up with Senator Riyo Chuchi to aid the new chairman in recovering his family.

EP. 5 "CORRUPTION"

EP. 6 "THE ACADEMY"

Padmé Amidala, on a diplomatic mission to Mandalore, and Duchess Satine Kryze uncover something sinister beneath the planet's serene facade. Moogan smugglers are sneaking in supplies, including bottled tea destined for the Mandalorian schools. To increase their profits, they have been diluting the tea with a hazardous chemical.

Meanwhile Ahsoka Tano is assigned to teach a class at a leadership academy on Mandalore. Inspired by the class, Duchess Satine's zealous nephew – Korkie Kryze – and his classmates uncover the nefarious plot. Prime Minister Almec is part of the black market conspiracy on Mandalore, so he attempts to silence Duchess Satine and the cadets before they expose his corruption.

EP. 7 "ASSASSIN"

While protecting Padmé Amidala during a political mission to Alderaan, Ahsoka Tano is plagued by recurring visions of presumed dead bounty hunter, Aurra Sing. Ultimately, Padmé narrowly avoids death when Sing attempts to assassinate her, and Ahsoka defends her.

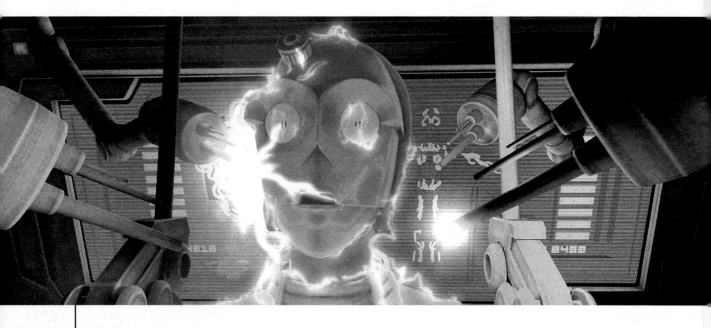

DATA & TRIVIA

- Dialogue in "Evil Plans" indicates that **C-3PO** previously worked for the chief negotiator in the Manakron system. This supports George Lucas' original notes saying that the golden droid was over 100 years old in *A New Hope*. That means Anakin (in *The Phantom Menace*) did not build the droid from scratch, but rebuilt an older droid that had previous protocol assignments. (Also note that Quinlan Vos starred in many *Star Wars* Dark Horse comics, which are now considered "Legends" material.)

EP. 8 "EVIL PLANS"

EP. 9 "HUNT FOR ZIRO"

On a routine shopping trip, C-3PO and R2-D2 are abducted by bounty hunter Cad Bane, who is looking for information about Coruscant's Senate building. Bane is part of a plot by the Hutt families to free Ziro the Hutt, who holds potentially damaging information about their illegal activities. (Note: The second chapter of this arc is actually Season One, Episode 22: "Hostage Crisis".)

Cad Bane has broken Ziro the Hutt out of prison. The Hutt Council demands that Ziro tell them where he's hidden vital – and incriminating – information. Ziro makes another daring escape with the help of his old flame, Sy Snootles. Bane is on Ziro's trail. Obi-Wan Kenobi and arrogant Jedi Quinlan Vos need to find him, too. A chase through the swamps of Nal Hutta leads them to Ziro's enormous mother, Mama the Hutt, who points them toward another secret...

EP. 10 "HEROES ON BOTH SIDES"

Padmé Amidala and Ahsoka Tano travel in secret to Raxus, the capital of the Confederacy of Independent Systems. While Amidala attempts to forge a peace agreement with the Separatists. For the first time, Ahsoka sees the people of the Confederacy, and finds many respectable characters.

EP. 11 "PURSUIT OF PEACE"

Padmé Amidala, Bail Organa, and Onaconda Farr attempt to rally senators in opposition to a bill that would appropriate funds for millions of new clone troops and have disastrous financial consequences for the Republic. Their opposition makes them targets for intimidation. After escaping two hired thugs in a harrowing speeder bike chase, Padmé is able to sway the Senate.

EP. 12 "NIGHTSISTERS"

EP. 13 "MONSTER"

EP. 14 "WITCHES OF THE MIST"

Troubled by Asajj Ventress' growing powers, Darth Sidious commands Count Dooku to eliminate her. But Ventress survives Dooku's assassination attempt, and the jilted apprentice vows revenge. She asks her kinswomen on Dathomir -- the mystical Nightsisters – for help. Mother Talzin, leader of the Nightsisters, veils Asajj and her fellow assassins in a cloak of invisibility, and they infiltrate Dooku's palace on Serenno. Though they fail to kill Dooku, their use of captured Jedi lightsabers leads the Sith Lord to mistakenly believe that the Jedi have tried to kill him. Wanting protection, he, too, asks Mother Talzin for help: a new apprentice.

DATA & TRIVIA

- The title for "Heroes on Both Sides" is pulled directly from the opening crawl for *Revenge of the Sith*.

Ventress and her kin seize the opportunity for more revenge. Ventress visits the Nightbrothers on the far side of Dathomir and discovers the most brutal and powerful warrior among them: Savage Opress. With her dark magic powers, Talzin transforms Savage into a hulking warrior loyal to Ventress. She then delivers Opress to Dooku, where he will serve as his apprentice until called upon by the Nightsisters.

Anakin Skywalker and Obi-Wan Kenobi, sent to track down the mysterious figure behind the deaths of several Jedi, soon find themselves on the trail of Opress, now trained in the ways of the Sith. When Opress returns to Dooku after an unsuccessful assignment, Ventress strikes. Calling on Opress, they attack Dooku, but Opress' loyalty is fleeting. Ventress discovers that he has a will of his own.

When Opress returns to Mother Talzin, she gives him a new task: to search the Outer Rim for his long-lost brother....

DATA & TRIVIA

- Mother Talzin, the spiritual guide of Dathomir's Nightsisters, sells the services her magic to the galaxy's wealthy and powerful. Long before the Clone Wars, Darth Sidious had promised to make Talzin his right hand, only to renege on his promise and steal her son, Darth Maul, to train as his apprentice.

EP. 15 "OVERLORDS"

EP. 16 "ALTAR OF MORTIS"

EP. 17 "GHOSTS OF MORTIS"

A mysterious force draws Anakin Skywalker, Obi-Wan Kenobi, and Ahsoka Tano to a distant planet. Its sole inhabitants are a family of exceptionally powerful Force-wielders, who attempt to determine whether Anakin is truly the Chosen One. The patriarch, known only as the Father, has spent ages maintaining the balance between the Daughter, who is strong with the light side of the Force, and the Son, aligned with the dark side. The Father is dying,

however, and wants Anakin to perhaps take his place to keep the balance.

The Son takes Ahsoka captive and puts her under the spell of the dark side in an attempt to entice Anakin into joining him. The Daughter breaks the forbidden rule by taking Obi-Wan to the Altar of Mortis, wherein a dagger is kept that is capable of killing a Force-wielder.

The Son renews his efforts to convert Anakin. He shows Anakin images of his dark future, and promises him the power to avert this destiny. The Father recognizes that the Son has broken the rules of time. He wipes Anakin's memory of these future visions, and steals the Mortis Dagger to end the conflict.

DATA & TRIVIA

- **The Force** is a mysterious energy field created by life that binds the galaxy together. By harnessing the power of the Force, Jedi, Sith, and others sensitive to this spiritual energy may obtain extraordinary abilities: levitating objects, influencing the minds of others or even seeing things before they happen. While the Force can grant users powerful abilities, it also directs their actions. It has a will of its own, which both scholars and mystics have spent millennia seeking to understand.

- Liam Neeson and Pernilla August reprised their roles from *The Phantom Menace*. Neeson returned as Qui-Gon Jinn, while August was once again the calming voice of Anakin's mother, Shmi (both characters appear in visions).

DATA & TRIVIA

- Stephen Stanton provided **Tarkin's voice**—a role originated by Peter Cushing in *A New Hope*, followed by Wayne Pygram in *Star Wars: Revenge of the Sith* (2005) and Guy Henry in *Rogue One: A Star Wars Story* (2016).

EP. 18 **"THE CITADEL"**

EP. 19 **"COUNTERATTACK"**

EP. 20 **"CITADEL RESCUE"**

With help from R2-D2 and a squad of captured battle droids, a team of Jedi and clone troopers led by Obi-Wan Kenobi and Anakin Skywalker attempt to free Jedi Master Even Piell from a high-security Separatist prison on Lola Sayu. Piell is the only one who knows about the Nexus Route, knowledge that could decide who wins the war. Defying orders, Ahsoka Tano tags along.

They liberate Piell and his fleet officer, Captain Wilhuff Tarkin, from their cells. Escaping from the

Citadel means evading traps and pitfalls; everyone must work in tandem to survive. Their attempt to board a shuttle fails when heavy weapons fire destroys it. Trooper Echo apparently dies in the blast. They flee to the caves and send a rescue call to the Jedi Temple on Coruscant.

Anakin and Obi-Wan then lead the escaped prisoners across the planet's dangerous landscape. Above, Plo Koon leads a task force through the Separatist defenses. Below, Piell is ravaged by wolf-like anooba tracking beasts; before he dies, he passes on the Nexus Routes coordinates to Ahsoka.

When the survivors finally return to Coruscant, Ahsoka refuses to disclose her intel to anyone but the Jedi Council, while Tarkin refuses to hand over his half to anyone other than Supreme Chancellor Palpatine.

EP. 21 "PADAWAN LOST"

EP. 22 "WOOKIEE HUNT"

Ahsoka Tano and a group of abducted younglings are trapped on the Trandoshan moon, Wasskah—where they become unwilling prey in a cruel hunt led by Garnac. The younglings lose all hope, despite the best efforts of their spirited leader, Kalifa, before Ahsoka rallies them to strike back against the Trandoshans.

Ahsoka and her youngling allies are still struggling to evade the hunters when they receive an unexpected boost: a new captive arrives, Chewbacca the Wookiee. Chewie scrounges parts from a wrecked slave ship to assemble a communicator. Help arrives in the towering, shaggy form of Wookiee warriors led by General Tarfful.

FAMOUS BATTLES

1. A bounty hunter has to be prepared for any battle, often relying on technology to counter the abilities of adversaries and Force users.

2. Powered by Sith sorcery, Savage Opress becomes the latest threat facing the Jedi Order.

3. In her final battle as a warrior for the Sith, Asajj Ventress is pushed to the edge – cornered and abandoned by those she trusted.

4. Few in the galaxy are as merciless and cold blooded as Cad Bane, a bounty hunter who doesn't care if his target is a man, woman, or even a child...

4.

SEASON 4
EPISODE GUIDE

EP. 1 **"WATER WAR"**

EP. 2 **"GUNGAN ATTACK"**

EP. 3 **"PRISONERS"**

When the king of Mon Cala is assassinated, talks break down between the Mon Calamari people and the Quarren, co-inhabitants of an aquatic world. To stop a civil war, the Republic sends Padmé Amidala and Anakin Skywalker to work with Captain Ackbar; unbeknownst to them, the Quarren are already being backed by the Separatists, led by the shark-like Riff Tamson. The Jedi wind up protecting Mon Cala's new leader, the young Prince Lee-Char, from the attack.

Anakin and the rest of his team are overrun; Lee-Char and Ahsoka Tano must evade capture on their own. Yoda calls upon the amphibious Gungan Grand Army to help. Tamson doubles his efforts to track

down Lee-Char by unleashing reinforcements given to him by Count Dooku—*Trident* drilling gunships.

Republic and Gungan forces are captured by Riff Tamson and his Karkarodon enforcers. It is up to Ahsoka and Lee-Char to unite the fractured people of Mon Cala and drive out the Separatist invaders.

EP. 4 "SHADOW WARRIOR"

The Gungans are being tricked into siding with Count Dooku and the Separatists against the Naboo. When

Padmé Amidala and Anakin Skywalker arrive to put things back in order, General Grievous is taken prisoner by the Gungans, but Anakin is taken prisoner by Dooku. Padmé must choose between them.

DATA & TRIVIA

- A strange, alien-built combat vessel used to deploy large numbers of troops, the **Trident-class assault ship** is part of the Separatist fleet of battle craft. The squid-shaped vehicle can "swim" through space with the help of engines concealed within its trailing tentacles. When it closes in on an enemy ship, it can blast it apart with laser weaponry or grapple the vessel in an unbreakable tentacle grip.

- The title **"Shadow Warrior"** is a nod to the English translation of *Kagemusha*, a 1980 Akira Kurosawa film executive produced by George Lucas.

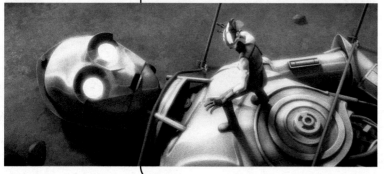

After groundquakes devastate the planet Aleen, a Republic relief effort arrives, including R2-D2 and C-3PO. When the natives' pleas go unheard, the droids happen to fall through a hole into Aleen's surreal subterranean world where they learn about the fracture between the two worlds.

Forced to escape a Separatist attack in a Y-wing fighter, the droids visit the world of the Patitite Pattuna, where they encounter tiny natives and are forced to fight in a gladiatorial arena aboard a pirate ship on the planet Balnab.

DATA & TRIVIA

- A rocky, temperate world found in the Mid Rim of the galaxy, **Aleen** is known for its friendly, boisterous natives, the Aleena, who have traveled throughout the galaxy. Beneath Aleen's ground are other civilizations, unknown to the surface world or to the Republic.

- "The General" is directed by Walter Murch, legendary editor and sound designer, who worked with George Lucas on *THX 1138* (1971) and *American Graffiti* (1973).

Anakin Skywalker is forced to turn over command of his clone troopers, the 501st Legion, to a new commander, Jedi Master Pong Krell. Tensions run high as Krell makes the already deadly mission to capture the gloomy capital of Umbara even more dangerous.

Krell orders Captain Rex and the troopers to attack a heavily fortified Umbaran airbase. It is a certain suicide mission, unless the clones use their ingenuity—but they are on the edge of mutiny.

After the clones manage to conquer the airbase, General Krell orders the 501st to continue toward the fortified capital. Krell cares nothing about casualties. Realizing there's a better plan, several clone troopers instead carry out a rogue, covert operation.

With two of his men, Fives and Jesse, facing execution for disobeying orders, Captain Rex must confront the overly aggressive Krell. Rex must make a hard choice as standing against his general would be an act of mutiny.

EP. 11 **"KIDNAPPED"**

EP. 12 **"SLAVES OF THE REPUBLIC"**

EP. 13 **"ESCAPE FROM KADAVO"**

Zygerrian slavers, working for the Separatists, invade Kiros. Anakin Skywalker and Ahsoka Tano rush to the planet and find that the slavers have abducted an entire colony of people and planted a network of bombs. To save the day, Obi-Wan Kenobi must fight their imposing leader, Darts D'Nar.

DATA & TRIVIA

- This Besalisk Jedi named **Pong Krell** won many battles and has an unshakable confidence. However, the casualty rates of the clone troopers under his command are extremely high. In personal combat, he is ferocious: his massive arms carry two double-ended lightsabers!

- Although double-bladed lightsabers have been carried by others, including Darth Maul, Pong Krell is the first Jedi to have a hinged double-ended lightsaber. The hinged style of lightsaber was showcased again in *The Rise of Skywalker*, when Rey witnesses a vision of her possible future as a Sith.

To locate the missing colonists and prevent them from being sold into slavery, Anakin, Obi-Wan, and Ahsoka then go undercover to infiltrate the Zygerrian gangs. Anakin struggles with his emotions as a wily Zygerrian queen, Miraj Scintel, forces him to take questionable actions at a slave auction in order to carry out his mission.

Anakin tries to convince the queen that she too is a slave and a pawn in the Separatist plot masterminded by Count Dooku. Meanwhile, Obi-Wan toils in the slave camps of Kadavo, where he is to be executed…

DATA & TRIVIA

- "Kidnapped," "Slave of the Republic" and "Escape from Kadavo" were adapted from Dark Horse Comics' six-issue story arc, **"Slaves of the Republic."**

EP. 14 **"A FRIEND IN NEED"**

A peace conference on Mandalore between Separatists and Republic delegates is interrupted by Lux Bonteri, the son of a late Separatist senator, who accuses Count Dooku of murdering his mother. Ahsoka Tano saves Lux from death, but then finds out he's joined the Death Watch warriors.

EP. 15 "DECEPTION"

EP. 16 "FRIENDS AND ENEMIES"

EP. 17 "THE BOX"

EP. 18 "CRISIS ON NABOO"

When the Jedi learn of a Separatist plot to kidnap Supreme Chancellor Palpatine, Obi-Wan Kenobi must go deep undercover. He even fakes his own death, not even telling Anakin Skywalker, before posing as a hardened criminal to get information from conspirators in prison.

Disguised as bounty hunter Rako Hardeen, Obi-Wan travels across the galaxy to Hutt Space with fugitives Cad Bane and Moralo Eval, still hoping to discover their plans. They are pursued by Anakin and Ahsoka Tano, who have no idea they're chasing their Jedi friend.

The disguised Obi-Wan then voyages with Bane and Eval to Serenno, where they engage in a brutal competition with other bounty hunters from around the galaxy in the Box to determine whom Count Dooku will hire to assassinate the chancellor.

When the chancellor travels to Naboo to preside over a public ceremony, the Festival of Light, he is guarded by Jedi Knights. Nevertheless Dooku and his bounty hunters, including an undercover Obi-Wan Kenobi, then launch their assassination plan.

DATA & TRIVIA

- **Sio Bibble** is a character who first appeared in the theatrical release of *The Phantom Menace*.

DATA & TRIVIA

- Designed by criminal mastermind Moralo Eval, **the Box** is a lethal simulator designed to test beings on their deadly skills. Hidden inside Count Dooku's palace on his home world of Serreno, the Box is the ultimate challenge for bounty hunters.

EP. 19 **"MASSACRE"**

EP. 20 **"BOUNTY"**

Count Dooku, determined to punish the Nightsisters of Dathomir, orders General Grievous to launch an all-out droid attack against the magic-wielding witches. Mother Talzin and Asajj Ventress lead the defense with the dark powers at their command—which include summoning the dead.

The Nightsisters are defeated. A wandering Ventress joins a team of bounty hunters under the leadership of young Boba Fett. On the planet Quarzite, they undertake a dangerous but profitable mission on a subtram that tests the strength of Ventress' character.

EP. 21 **"BROTHERS"**

EP. 22 **"REVENGE"**

Dark warrior Savage Opress is on a quest to find his long-lost brother, Maul. Could Maul truly be alive, given that a decade has passed since his gruesome bisection at the hands of Obi-Wan Kenobi? Savage voyages to the depths of a junkyard planet, Lotho Minor, on the trail of the fallen Sith Lord.

Savage finds Maul, and revives him; the brothers are reunited. They pursue Obi-Wan in search of revenge, forcing him into a surprising alliance.

DATA & TRIVIA

- Industrial Light & Magic art director **Aaron McBride** designed Maul's cyborg form in his story for the graphic novel *Star Wars: Visionaries*, published by Dark Horse in 2005.

1.

FAMOUS BATTLES

1. Obi-Wan Kenobi knowingly walks into Maul's trap, as he has no choice but to face the monster that killed his master.

3. Time is precious on the planet Kiros as Anakin Skywalker and his Padawan Ahsoka Tano battle through a droid army in a desperate attempt to defuses several bombs.

3. Feeling shut out by the Jedi Council, Anakin Skywalker's emotions run close to the surface in a tense battle against the Separatist forces.

SEASON 5
EPISODE GUIDE

EP. 2 **"A WAR ON TWO FRONTS"**

EP. 3 **"FRONT-RUNNERS"**

EP. 4 **"THE SOFT WAR"**

EP. 4 **"TIPPING POINTS"**

Anakin Skywalker, Obi-Wan Kenobi, Ahsoka Tano and Captain Rex travel to Onderon, a planet under Separatist control. There, they train a group of insurgent rebels in secret – including Lux Bonteri – to help take back the capital city of Iziz from the rule of a duplicitous king.

Under Ahsoka's command, Onderon rebels infiltrate the capital and carry out a series of strikes. As the king comes under increasing pressure to deal with the growing crisis, the rebels fight about who should be their leader—just before launching their most daring venture.

After the rebels, lead by Steela Gerrera, attempt to rescue Onderon's true king, Ramsis Dendup, the Separatist-controlled King Rash orders his execution. As a full-scale revolt embroils the capital Iziz and spreads to surrounding cities, King Rash sends in droid gunships to destroy the rebels. The price for victory escalates...

DATA & TRIVIA

- In the Onderon arc, the **planet Onderon** comes from a story set thousands of years before the Clone Wars told in the *Tales of the Jedi* comic book series (1993).

- **Gregg Berger,** who performs the voice of General Kalani in "The Soft War" and "Tipping Points," also portrayed the character in the *Star Wars Rebels'* Season Three episode, "The Last Battle."

EP. 6 **"THE GATHERING"**

EP. 7 **"A TEST OF STRENGTH"**

EP. 8 **"BOUND FOR RESCUE"**

EP. 9 **"A NECESSARY BOND"**

Ahsoka Tano escorts a group of younglings to Ilum for "the Gathering," during which they learn from Yoda and undergo a crucial rite of passage: the construction of their lightsabers from the living crystals found on that planet. The younglings must also grapple with both physical and inner challenges as they face the potentially dangerous task.

On the return trip from Ilum in the *Crucible*, Ahsoka and her younglings are attacked by Hondo Ohnaka's pirate gang, who want to steal the valuable kyber crystals. The children must use ingenious and improvised traps to thwart the brigands.

DATA & TRIVIA

- In "The Gathering," **kyber crystals** are colorless until a young Jedi holds it, upon which it becomes attuned to the Force-user. This appears to be what decides the color of Jedi lightsaber blades.

Ahsoka Tano is captured by the pirates, and the younglings have to work together to infiltrate the pirates' den, using their wits and courage to deceive Ohnaka.

The situation becomes dire when General Grievous launches a full-scale attack on the pirate base on Florrum—to avenge the pirates' emprisonment of Count Dooku. Ahsoka and the younglings decide to fight side-by-side with Hondo and his pirates to turn back the Separatist forces.

DATA & TRIVIA

- In "A Test of Strength," design of the **lightsaber assembly** was inspried by the "Build Your Own Lightsaber" activity center at the Star Trader shop in Disney parks.

- In "A Necessary Bond," **Boba Fett's starship** makes its first appearance since "Lethal Trackdown," the Season Two finale. In that episode the ship still had Jango Fett's paint scheme. Hondo Ohnaka repainted it with the colors it will have when seen in *Star Wars: The Empire Strikes Back* (1980).

- The most sacred world to the Jedi Order is the **ancient planet Ilum,** which is encased in ice and whipped by chilling winds. Hidden beneath the frozen surface is a Jedi temple from the very dawn of the Order. Within the legendary Crystal Caves Jedi initiates undergo the Gathering.

EP. 10 **"SECRET WEAPONS"**

EP. 11 **"A SUNNY DAY IN THE VOID"**

EP. 12 **"MISSING IN ACTION"**

EP. 13 **"POINT OF NO RETURN"**

R2-D2 is one of a team of five Republic droids—"D-Squad"—chosen for an important mission. They are led by the diminutive Colonel Meebur Gascon, and must obtain an encryption module from a Separatist dreadnought.

After a comet swarm damages their shuttle, R2, Colonel Gascon, and the other droids crash-land on a desolate planet. In dire straits, they must make their way across a bewildering deserted expanse knowns as the Void in order to carry out their mission.

In a nearly vacant town called Pons Ora, R2 and his team find a clone commando named Gregor who is suffering from amnesia. Gascon wants to unlock Gregor's mind, because he hopes it might help their mission.

D-Squad finally escapes the planet Abafar aboard a Jedi Cruiser—but then must stop saboteurs aboard their ship who plan on destroying a crucial Republic conference on the space station Valor.

DATA & TRIVIA

- The opening logo for the episodes of this arc are blue rather than yellow—a tribute to R2-D2.

- The **Carida system** seen in "Point of No Return" first appeared in *The Jedi Academy Trilogy* "Legends" novels by Kevin J. Anderson (circa 1994). The look of Valor station was inspired by the departure station in the recently revamped Star Tours:

The Adventures Continue ride at Disneyland and Disney World.

- In "Missing in Action," several posters in the background of some interiors are homages to classic **LucasArts adventure video games:** Kowakian Monkey Island, Full Throttle (with a swoop bike), and Day of the Sarlacc instead of Day of the Tentacle.

DATA & TRIVIA

- In "Revival," the background of Hondo's camp is a superstructure with the words "Hondo's Salvage - prices slashed" in Aurebesh.

- During the Clone Wars, **Pre Vizsla** serves as governor of Concordia, a moon of Mandalore, and appears to be a close ally of Duchess Satine Kryze. But Vizsla has another, secret life—as leader of Death Watch, a group of Mandalorian commandos who want to take control of the planet. Vizsla despises Satine's pacifist beliefs and longs to restore Mandalore's warrior heritage.

Fueled by vengeance and rage, newly reunited brothers Savage Opress and Maul spread terror and violence across the galaxy. The Sith duo recruit Hondo Ohnaka and his pirates to form a criminal empire—but Obi-Wan Kenobi and Adi Gallia are in pursuit.

Savage and Maul, nearly defeated, are rescued by Pre Vizsla's Death Watch. They forge an alliance to take over Mandalore; Maul wants to create an army of underworld thugs, and Death Watch commandos.

Backed by a criminal network, the Sith brothers and Death Watch launch an attack on Mandalore. However, the leaders of the attack are also plotting against each other.

Maul ends up on the throne of Mandalore. Continuing his rampage, he uses Duchess Satine Kryze as bait to lure Obi-Wan into a trap. Darth Sidious watches the proceedings with interest...

DATA & TRIVIA

- The **Black Sun** criminal syndicate in "Eminence" originated in Lucasfilm's multimedia Legends story, *Shadows of the Empire*, released in 1996.

DATA & TRIVIA

- The four episodes of the of **Ahsoka Tano's arc** are named after classic Alfred Hitchcock films: *Sabotage* (1936); *The Man Who Knew Too Much* (1934, remake 1956); *To Catch a Thief* (1955); and *The Wrong Man* (1956).

- Among the joke stops on the subtram map in "To Catch a Jedi" are "North Hollywood," "Big Rock Ranch," "Letterman" (Lucasfilm's offices in San Francisco), "Lucasville," and "Filoniville."

EP. 17 **"SABOTAGE"**

EP. 18 **"THE JEDI WHO KNEW TOO MUCH"**

EP. 19 **"TO CATCH A JEDI"**

EP. 20 **"THE WRONG JEDI"**

Anakin Skywalker and Ahsoka Tano investigate a deadly bombing at the Jedi Temple. Rumors say that a Jedi might be the saboteur.

When the Republic military takes over the Temple bombing case, Ahsoka finds herself at odds with Admiral Tarkin. She is increasingly under suspicion of being the bomber herself.

Ahsoka becomes a fugitive and escapes to the criminal underworld of Coruscant, where she forms an unlikely alliance.

She is nevertheless caught, and, on trial for murder, faces her greatest challenge. Ahsoka is expelled from the Jedi Order. Only Anakin believes her innocent—and searches for the real culprit…

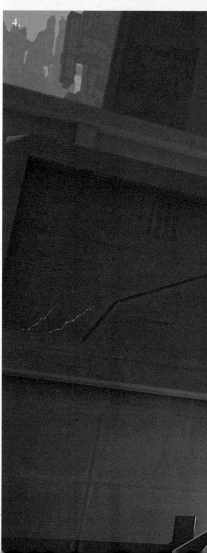

FAMOUS BATTLES

1. The mercurial Hondo Ohnaka didn't plan on kidnapping a bunch of younglings, but he's not going to ignore the opportunity either.

2. Fueled by the galactic war raging through the systems, Mandalore's civil war tears the planet of warriors apart.

3. As the war takes it's toll on the Republic, the manipulations of the Sith drive Ahsoka Tano from Anakin Skywalker and the Republic.

4. Discarded by the Sith, hunted by the Jedi, Maul has only his brother to turn to – a weakness that Darth Sidious is more than happy to exploit.

2.

SEASON 6
EPISODE GUIDE

Clone trooper Tup succumbs to a mysterious mental illness that results in the death of a Jedi Master. Unable to account for his murderous actions, Tup is sedated and sent back to Kamino for examination.

In the sterile laboratories of Kamino, the ailing Tup and Fives are quarantined. With the help of medical droid AZI-3, Fives uncovers a secret buried deep within the Republic's cloning program.

After he dies, the body of Tup is scheduled for transport to Coruscant, where Supreme Chancellor Palpatine's own doctors will closely examine it. Fives breaks protocol and discovers that there is an organic construct of unknown purpose hidden in the brains of all the clone troopers.

Fives continues to push for answers regarding the clone contamination and secures an audience with Chancellor Palpatine. But the situation worsens when Fives is accused of attacking the chancellor, and must flee deep into the Coruscant cityscape, pursued by his fellow clone troopers.

DATA & TRIVIA

- The **Grand Republic Medical Facility** is the same towering structure seen at end of *Revenge of the Sith*, where Darth Vader is born. The room where Fives is examined is more of an operating theater, however, and not the same room as in the movie.

EP. 5 **"AN OLD FRIEND"**

EP. 6 **"THE RISE OF CLOVIS"**

EP. 7 **"CRISIS AT THE HEART"**

While on Scipio to fund a mercy mission, Padmé Amidala is called upon by an old friend, Rush Clovis, who needs her help to uncover corruption in the Banking Clan. They must evade bounty hunter Embo to escape the planet with the incriminating info.

Back on Coruscant, Clovis – now considered a traitor to the Republic – makes a dubious deal that puts him at the head of the Banking Clan. Anakin Skywalker's increasing hatred of Clovis strains his relationship with Padmé.

Clovis' deal with the Separatists then backfires with disastrous consequences...

EP. 8 **"THE DISAPPEARED, PART I"**

EP. 9 **"THE DISAPPEARED, PART II"**

The peaceful world of Bardotta and its mystic ways are threatened by an ancient prophecy: Its top spiritual leaders are vanishing. Queen Julia calls for help from her most trusted friend in the Senate—Jar Jar Binks. Recognizing the importance of Bardotta's spiritual balance, the Jedi Council sends Mace Windu to accompany Binks and investigate.

Queen Julia is abducted by the bloodthirsty Frangawl cult to fulfill a dark rite. Jar Jar and Mace must find the missing queen before the dark side grows in strength.

DATA & TRIVIA

- "The Disappeared, Part I" marks the first *Star Wars: The Clone Wars* appearance of serpentine **Oppo Rancisis** on the Jedi Council, first seen in *The Phantom Menace*, but left off of the council till now.

- The **planet Bardotta** appears in this arc, and was named in reference to the famous French actress Brigitte Bardot.

EP. 10 "THE LOST ONE" / EP. 11 "VOICES"

EP. 12 "DESTINY" / EP. 13 "SACRIFICE"

During a Jedi mission, a lightsaber belonging to long-dead master Sifo-Dyas is found, which prompts Yoda, Obi-Wan Kenobi, and Anakin Skywalker to begin an investigation into his decade-old disappearance. Darth Sidious orders Darth Tyranus (aka Count Dooku) to clean up any loose ends that may lead the Jedi to discover the truth of the Sith conspiracy.

Yoda is deeply unsettled when he hears something from beyond the grave: the voice of Qui-Gon Jinn. Knowing that it's impossible for a Jedi to retain his identity after death, the Jedi Council begins to worry that Yoda may be corrupted by the dark side. Yoda flees the Jedi Temple to follow the disembodied voice.

DATA & TRIVIA

- "The Lost One" shows the moment when the Jedi finally discover Count Dooku's Sith name, Darth Tyranus, and realize that **Tyranus/Dooku** was in reality Jango Fett's mysterious patron in *Attack of the Clones*—the Sith/Jedi who financed the creation of the millions of clone troopers.

- **Yoda's vision** in "Voices" features the future confrontation between Darth Sidious and the Jedi in *Revenge of the Sith*; also visible is the death of Shaak Ti, killed by General Grievous, which was edited out of that film.

Letting the Force guide him, Yoda voyages to the heart of the galaxy and an ancient world that is one of the wellsprings of the Force and the source of midi-chlorians. Yoda undergoes difficult trials administered by the Five Priestesses, mysterious Force-wielders who hold the secret to immortality.

After the trials, Yoda travels to the Sith homeworld of Moraband, where he must face an ancient evil determined to rule the galaxy...

DATA & TRIVIA

- "Destiny" bridges the character of **Yoda**, the battlefield general of the prequels, to the more spiritual Yoda of the original trilogy, who belittles war.

- In "Destiny," Jedi Yoda has an idyllic vision of **Jedi** gathered on the Temple training grounds: among them are Quinlan Vos, Saesee Tiin, Mace Windu, Ahsoka Tano, Tera Sinube, Aayla Secura, Anakin Skywalker, Kit Fisto, Eeth Koth, Ki-Adi-Mundi, Shaak Ti, Adi Gallia, Barriss Offee, Obi-Wan Kenobi, Qui-Gon Jinn, and Dooku.

DATA & TRIVIA

• A member of the Jedi Council years before the Clone Wars, **Sifo-Dyas** believed the galaxy would soon be at war, and advocated for the Republic to create an army for its defense. After the Jedi Order rejected his ideas and removed him from the council, he secretly contacted the Kaminoans and commissioned them to create a clone army, which he led the Kaminoans to believe was for the Republic. In doing so, Sifo-Dyas became an pawn of the Sith, who took over the project and hired the Pyke Syndicate to murder Sifo-Dyas on Oba Diah's moon. A decade after Sifo-Dyas' death, Obi-Wan Kenobi discovered the army on Kamino. The Jedi then took control of this army on Supreme Chancellor Palpatine's orders, setting the Clone Wars in motion.

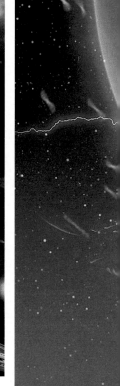

FAMOUS BATTLES

1. Though his battle with Darth
    Sidious occurs within a vision, the
    influence and danger of this mental
    projection of the Dark Lord is
    very real.

2. The Separatists attack Ringo Vinda
    in an attempt to seize the clone Tup,
    who has suffered a breakdown of
    mysterious origin.

3. The Nightsister known as Mother
    Talzin attempts to renew herself by
    siphoning off the living Force from
    the Bardottan Queen.

1.

SEASON 7
EPISODE GUIDE

On the planet Anaxes, the Separatists, lead by Admiral Trench, are attacking one of the Republic's largest shipyards, and the droid army are dangerously close to taking control. To combat the threat, Captain Rex and Commander Cody team up with Hunter, Tech, Wrecker, and Crosshair, who are all members of the experimental unit Clone Force 99, known as the Bad Batch, to infiltrate the Separatist's cyber center. Upon gaining access, Tech uncovers a live signal coming from another planet, Skako Minor, that continually repeats "CT-1409" in a voice that sounds like ARC trooper Echo's, Rex's fallen comrade.

Along with Anakin Skywalker and the Bad Batch, Captain Rex heads to Skako Minor to trace the signal and determine how the Separatists are predicting the Republic's strategies. The team make their way to the city of Purkoll to infiltrate the Separatist's tower base, and during the assault, they ascend to a chamber where the origin of the signal is coming from. Tech and Rex discover a coffin-like stasis chamber holding Echo and release him; he falls forward toward Rex, a gaunt and pale shadow of his former self. The Separatist's Techno Union has been "plugged" into him in order to steal the Republic's battle plans.

After rescuing Echo, Skywalker, Rex, and the Bad Batch have to escape Skako Minor while being hounded by countless battle droids. On the run with seemingly no viable route to take, the clones attract keeradaks, reptile-like flying creatures indigenous to the planet, by playing a recording of the creature's own distress call. With the enemy hot on their tail, the clones and Skywalker jump onto keeradaks' backs and fly to safety.

Upon returning to Anaxes, Echo hatches a plan to end the Separatist threat, but his comrades are suspicious of his proposal. While Jedi Masters Mace Windu and Obi-Wan Kenobi lead an assault team to retake the assembly complex, Echo, Rex and the Bad Batch will infiltrate Admiral Trench's dreadnought above Anaxes and feed him false strategies in order to secure a Republic victory. After the ground assault seemingly haults the Separatist threat, Echo discovers there's a bomb hidden within the complex, and it's up to Windu to deactivate it. With help from Skywalker, Mace is able to disarm the device, averting a disaster that could have resulted the destruction of most of Anaxes.

Having found purpose again, Echo decides to leave his friends and comrades to take up Hunter's offer to join the Bad Batch.

DATA & TRIVIA

- In this arc, the **battle on Anaxes** is part of the "Outer Rim Sieges"— that is, the final campaign of the Clone Wars as mentioned by Obi-Wan Kenobi in *Revenge of the Sith*.

Since leaving the Jedi Order, Ahsoka Tano has been living a gypsy-like existence, traveling Coruscant on a rickety speeder bike. In the rough-and-tumble lower level 1313 of the city planet, he stumbles upon Trace Martez, an aspiring pilot struggling to get by, alongside her older sister, Rafa. Trace is willing to help Ahsoka—for a price. While getting to know each other, the three get into some hot water assembling a trio of dangerous droids.

After avoiding imminent disaster, Ahsoka intends to keep her Jedi past a secret and build a new life as a simple mechanic. Tano agrees to help her new friend Trace work on her ship. But Rafa's latest plan sends them to Kessel on a dangerous and illegal job to make some quick credits by running spice to Pyke Syndicate gangsters on Oba Diah. The jobs tests Ahsoka's moral and ethical beliefs as she tries to keep the sisters out of trouble. In a moment of panic, Trace dumps the cargo of spice while traveling through hyperspace, leaving the three of them in quite a predicament upon arrival.

The sisters and Ahsoka are taken prisoner by the Pyke's for failing to deliver their shipment. It is during captivity where Ahsoka learns that Trace and Rafa's parents were killed as a result of the Jedi attempting to apprehend a criminal, which caused the two to mistrust the Order. With no family, apart from each other, the sisters had no choice but to lean on each other for survival, something Ahsoka could relate to. However, this revelation gives Tano pause in telling the sisters about her Jedi past.

As the Pyke's continue to torture the sisters regarding the location of the missing spice, Trace escapes their clutches, only to run into Ahsoka and Rafa along the way, who have also broken out of their cell. During the ensuing pursuit through Oba Diah, the trio are observed from afar by three Mandalorians, among them Bo-Katan Kryze. Before long, Ahsoka and the sisters are recaptured by the Pykes.

Ahsoka makes a deal with Marg Krim, leader of the Pyke Syndicate, to let Trace and Rafa recover the dumped spice, while she remains hostage. The deal is all a ruse to enable the sisters to return home, but Rafa recognizes Tano's sacrifice and hatches a plan to return to Oba Diah and rescue the former Jedi. Meanwhile, Ahsoka escapes her cell and begins planting explosives all throughout the Pyke's complex. Along the way she overhears a conversation between Krim and former Sith apprentice Maul,

where she learns they are working together. Before being recaptured, Ahsoka is able to locate Maul's location and discovers he is on Mandalore.

The sisters return, only to be recaptured. As the three are readied for execution, Tano reveals her identity and Jedi past, just before the planted explosives detonate. After a daring escape and dogfight, they make it back to Coruscant. There, Bo-Katan and two other Mandalorians approach Ahsoka to ask for her and the Republic's help to capture Maul.

DATA & TRIVIA

- The eldest of two sisters, **Rafa Martez** runs a galactic laundry facility she won gambling. She makes her real living through illegal jobs with the denizens of the Coruscant underworld. Rafa and her sister, Trace, have learned that their survival depends on themselves.

Ahsoka Tano agrees to help Bo-Katan Kryze, and the two return to the Republic looking for help from Anakin Skywalker and Obi-Wan Kenobi in taking back Mandalore and capturing Maul. But a surprise attack on Coruscant draws the Jedi away. Still, Skywalker, ever loyal to his old Padawan, assigns Commander Rex and a new division of clone troopers to assist Ahsoka on her mission. Before parting ways, Anakin presents Tano a gift—her old lightsabers, which have been slightly modified and now glow blue.

As the siege of Mandalore begins, clone gunships, Mandalorians, and Ahsoka soar through the air against Maul's warriors, fighting their way to the planet's surface. In the sewer system below the city, Ahsoka and her clones are ambushed, with Maul emerging from the shadows to toy with her...

Maul tells Ahsoka about Darth Sidious, just as Rex and a handful of troopers arrive to help Tano, forcing Maul to retreat. Ahsoka reports back to Obi-Wan, mentioning the name Darth Sidious, and the latter explains he is the mysterious Sith Lord who orchestrated the Clone Wars. The only way to learn more about Sidious is to capture Maul, but Kenobi is unable to send reinforcements to help in the pursuit.

After learning more about Ahsoka by interrogating a clone trooper, Maul waits patiently in the Mandalore

throne room for her to arrive. When she does, Maul uses the knowledge he gained to tempt Ahsoka into joining him to defeat Sidious, and surprisingly she accepts. It is then she learns of Anakin's role in Sidious' master plan, and that the war on Mandalore was Maul's ploy to lure Kenobi and Skywalker there so Maul could kill Anakin and deprive Sidious of his coveted apprentice. Ahsoka refuses to believe Maul's claim, igniting another clash between the two that ends with Maul's capture.

While traveling to Coruscant aboard a Jedi cruiser, with Maul as prisoner, Darth Sidious initiates Order 66, activating all clone troopers secret programming to destroy the Jedi. In a desperate move, Ahsoka frees Maul so he can create chaos and enable her to time to escape before being killed by her former clone allies. In the process, Ahsoka subdues Commander Rex and removes his inhibitor chip, effectively halting the effects of Order 66. Once completed, the two work together to reach a shuttle to leave the now-crippled and doomed cruiser, which is caught in the gravitation pull of a nearby moon. But it is Maul who first reaches the intended craft, leaving Ahsoka and Rex behind to certain doom. Miraculously, the pair survive the ordeal by locating a functional Y-wing.

After landing on the moon's surface, Ahsoka and Rex create a make-shift graveyard to honor the lost lives of the clones aboard the cruiser. Ahsoka is now on her own again, left to truly fend for herself in a radically changed galaxy…

In an epilogue that takes place years later, Anakin Skywalker has become Darth Vader. While exploring the wreckage of the downed cruiser on the same arctic moon, he finds Ahsoka's lightsaber. In his cold heart, he knows she is alive.

FAMOUS BATTLES

1. Having renounced the Jedi order, Ahsoka leads the attack to free Mandalore from the clutches of Maul and Death Watch.

2. Death Watch supercommando Rook Kast leads the mandalorians loyal to the Shadow Collective against the forces of Bo-Katan Kryze.

3. Betrayed by the clones that had only moments earlier been those most loyal to her, Ahsoka discovers the sinister power of Order 66 first hand.

1.

2.

BEHIND THE SCENES OF
STAR WARS™
THE CLONE WARS™

1 /

1 / Creating three-
dimensional maquettes
of characters for a
television show is
rare, as it's an
expensive process.

2 / The clay maquette
of Anakin Skywalker
was used to test the
translation of two-
dimensional art into
3D designs.

"Begun, the Clone War has." Yoda utters those ominous words at the end of *Star Wars*: Episode II *Attack of the Clones* (2002). The the end of those wars was revealed in *Star Wars*: Episode III *Revenge of the Sith* (2005)—but what happened in-between? What battles were fought? What dramas unfolded? Those questions were answered by the animated episodic TV show *Star Wars: The Clone Wars*, which debuted in 2008.

Set between *Attack of the Clones* and *Revenge of the Sith*, *The Clone Wars* explored the conflict between the Republic and the Separatists, the former led by Jedi generals and their seemingly loyal clone troopers; the latter is led by Count Dooku and General Grievous and their limitless droid armies. Both sides, however, are being manipulated by a mysterious Sith Lord, Darth Sidious, who is also Supreme Chancellor Palpatine.

From the theatrical movie debut in 2008 to its then-final episodes released as "The Lost Missions" in 2014, *The Clone Wars* was driven by stories George Lucas wanted to tell. The show premiered seven years before *Star Wars: The Force Awakens* (2015), at a time when a new *Star Wars* trilogy was only a distant dream. When the episodes exploded onscreen—packed with epic battles and personal challenges for Anakin Skywalker, Padmé Amidala, Obi-Wan

Kenobi, Boba Fett, Mace Windu, Jar Jar Binks, C-3PO, R2-D2, Maul, and many other characters from the filmic saga—fans immediately embraced it.

At the heart of those stories were also new characters, clone troopers, aliens—but mainly Ahsoka Tano, Anakin's Padawan learner. As Ahsoka matured over the seasons, fans young and old identified with her growth and the difficult decisions she had to make about the Jedi Order and her beliefs.

In addition, because an animated series doesn't have the same time constraints as a film, *The Clone Wars* had the room to explore many different styles of storytelling, even those that wouldn't have a place in a feature film: clone trooper issues, droid-centric escapades, witches, explorations of the Force, myriad political affairs, and epidemics. All of that and more found places in the show thanks to Lucas and his interests.

Lucas and his production team's weekly doses of adventure, emotions, beautiful animation, memorable music, and extraordinary voice-over performances earned millions of admirers. *Star Wars: The Clone Wars* helped redefine television animation, with bigger budgets, technological breakthroughs, and by expanding the kind of stories an animated show for a general audience could tell.

GEORGE LUCAS

CREATOR

Star Wars mastermind George Lucas offers his thoughts about The Clone Wars film and animated series, and the episodic nature of the story.

For a lot of young fans, *The Clone Wars* served as their introduction to *Star Wars*. What are your thoughts on that new generation of kids who were introduced to the *Star Wars* saga through *The Clone Wars* animated series? It's obviously a different tone, but still has the drama and the characters. The TV series is exactly like the movies. Exactly. It's basically the movies only with cartoon characters. It's basically a dramatic series: there's a lot of action and a bit of humor. It runs along at the same level. It's unusual for an animated show, because it's not really a hardcore movie like say *Beowulf* (2007) and it's not a Pixar movie; it falls in-between a PG rating and a PG-13, because it (*Star Wars*) is a bit funny, yet hard-edged.

It also seems to show a little bit more of the clone characters as well.
Yeah, we got to introduce the clones, which we didn't do in the movies. Now they're main characters, and they really are central to the whole story. You can identify them and recognize who they are, so it's like *Band of Brothers* (2001, a World War II miniseries) only with Jedi (laughs).

Some of the episodes are stand-alone and some are two or three or even four-episode story arcs. But it's not like the current vogue of (episodic TV) where you actually have to watch the entire series in order to understand what's going on. This is an old-fashioned episodic show. We looked at a few episodes on the big screen and it looked so beautiful and great that we said, "Gee, we can make a feature just like this." So we did.

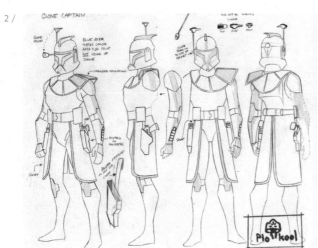

1 / *Star Wars* creator George Lucas.
2 / Early concept art of a clone trooper showcases the Phase I armor worn through the early episodes of the series.
3 / A clay maquette of a clone trooper, whose design would set the foundation for the entire Grand Army of the Republic.
4 / *Star Wars: The Clone Wars* theatrical release premiered on August 2008, with a budget of 8.5 million and a box office return of 68.3 million.

STAR
THE
CLONE
WARS
WARS

Executive Producer GEORGE LUCAS Director DAVE FILONI Producer CATHERINE WINDER
Writers HENRY GILROY STEVE MELCHING SCOTT MURPHY
Editor JASON TUCKER Score by KEVIN KINER Original Star Wars Themes and Score by JOHN WILLIAMS

LUCASFILM Ltd. PG PARENTAL GUIDANCE SUGGESTED IN THEATERS AUGUST 15 WARNER BROS. PICTURES
TM & © 2008 Lucasfilm Ltd. All Rights Reserved. Used Under Authorization.
www.starwars.com

HOW IT WAS MADE, PART I

Lucas had played with the idea of an animated Clone Wars television series for some time, in part due to his love for animation. Decades before, he had produced animated TV shows about C-3PO and R2-D2 as well as a show about the loveable Ewoks. When he decided to do the new series, Skywalker Ranch became its production hub. Just behind the Victorian-style Main House is the Carriage House: a three-story shingle-roof building, which became the bustling center of the new *Star Wars* chapter (it had formely been the home of Lucas Licensing).

Animation director of the prequel trilogy Rob Coleman was an early series director and animation consultant. He remembers, "There was this really wonderful, warm feeling the team had being on Skywalker Ranch. We were George's pet project; we were this special team. There was also a lot of trepidation, because we were taking on such a huge project, but there was great energy."

Production artists, technicians, and crew were recruited from all over the world to work on the show. One of the first hires was Alex Woo, who created designs for Anakin Skywalker, Obi-Wan Kenobi, and Count Dooku, among others. Producer Catherine Winder's challenge was to find a supervising director to head up the creative team. "George said he needed somebody who could look at things differently," says Winder, "who wouldn't be restrained by the traditional way of doing things, and who could come up with a look that was going to blow everybody away."

At an anime convention someone mentioned Dave Filoni as a candidate.

Filoni received a call not long afterward. He remembers, "I was like 'Clone Wars series at Lucasfilm Animation—yeah, right!'"

"He gave me the hardest time." Winder remembers. "Finally, I said, 'All right, because obviously you don't believe me, I'm going to hang up and you're going to feel really embarrassed.' At that moment Filoni realized the phone call was no prank. Then he got really nervous and started telling me how he was creating a Plo Koon costume in his garage (laughs). I almost did hang up on him!"

Eventually Filoni met with Lucas. "I didn't expect to get the job," Filoni says, "because George has worked with so many amazing artists over the years, like Ralph McQuarrie, Joe Johnston, Dennis Muren, and Phil Tippett, and I thought, *I don't have anything as great as those guys*. I figured it would be just a good experience and I would have a great story to tell."

"I was looking for a talented director," says Lucas, "who had a passion for *Star Wars* and understood the world in which it takes place. Dave came up with the kernel of a very different look for *The Clone Wars*. One that was very retro, but at the same time very cutting-edge."

After his meeting with Lucas, that same day, Winder offered Filoni the job. "It was really bizarre," Filoni says. "Suddenly, I was in charge of bringing this thing to life."

"He was already talking about characters," Coleman says, "shot composition, and telling a great story. He wanted to do the best job possible. I loved his energy."

1/

1/ A wire frame is used when sculpting a maquette. This serves as a form of skeleton, adding structure for the clay.
2 / Darren Marshall worked on *The Clone Wars* for 8 years, crafting both 3D maquettes as well as 2D artwork.

ep23 - Jocasta Nu - Orthos (flat color) - W. Lo - 08/01/07

HOW IT WAS MADE, PART II

The character design of *The Clone Wars* was soon defined by intense curves and angular graphic shapes rarely seen before in a CG cartoon. The artwork of Ralph McQuarrie, concept illustrator for the original trilogy, was also a great inspiration. Says Filoni, "We were intentionally carving angles into the characters, and using light and shadow to create graphic looks. Concept sculptor Darren Marshall really set the groundwork for what it was going to look like in 3D."

At another meeting with Lucas, Filoni showed him their designs photographed to stress the shadows and highlights. Marshall says, "I remember them taking the maquettes over to the Main House (at Skywalker Ranch), and it was like the three kings bringing gifts." "George pointed at the maquettes," Filoni remembers, "and said, 'This is good,' then he pointed at the photos

and goes, 'but this is great!' I breathed the biggest sigh of relief I think I've ever breathed."

One of the first, if not the first, writer to be recruited was Henry Gilroy, who worked closely with Filoni on ideas for the series. As early development began on the show, Lucas would come in to shape each episode in the editing room, and later he would establish their premises in writer meetings that prefaced each season.

Concurrently, many technological challenges were overcome, voice actors were hired, and a postproduction editing and sound crew was set up. Guest directors were invited to work on the show and creativity flowed.

Once broadcast on the Cartoon Network, out of the gate, *Star Wars: The Clone Wars* was a hit. Each subsequent year the series's fan base grew, with each season adding more amazing characters and deepening the story of the saga.

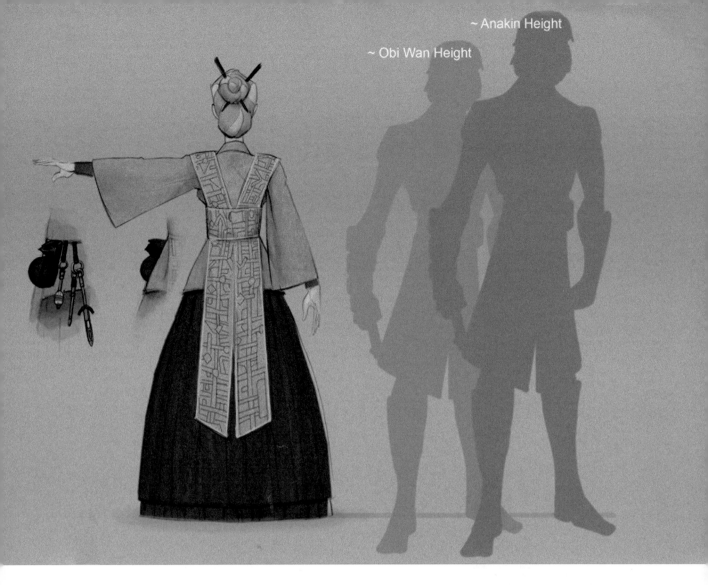

~ Anakin Height

~ Obi Wan Height

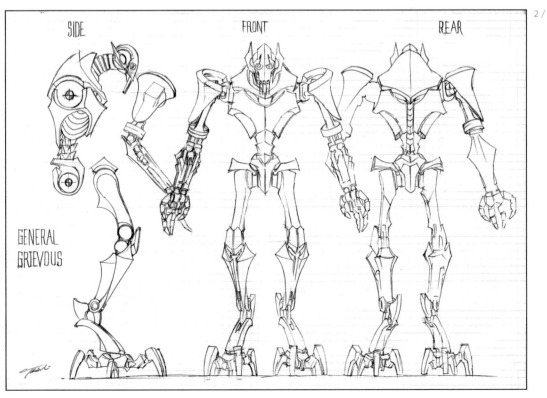

SIDE

FRONT

REAR

GENERAL GRIEVOUS

1 / The design for the Chief Librarian of the Jedi Archives, Jocasta Nu, follows the look of the same character as she appeared in the film *Attack of the Clones*, but also includes reference for her height in comparison to other characters.

1 / This two-dimensional concept art is used as a guide so that 3D animators can keep the design accurate from every possible angle.

DAVE FILONI
SUPERVISING DIRECTOR

What did Season Four represent technically and artistically for the production team? Everything. There's really nothing we couldn't do at that point. Creatively, we didn't have a situation where we ever say, "Let's not go to that type of planet. Let's not do that type of scenario. Let's not have thousands of people in a crowd." We didn't avoid things. We still had to be creative and figure out how to do it. We made creative choices as to how we were going to express visually the story that's being told. There are creative choices that have to be made

around the assets. I can't use this, so let's re-use this; let's re-purpose this. But in any movie franchise, that's what you have to do.

You saw it more in the 1970s and 1980s when they would re-use more things. Now it seems as if every feature film is about customization, so every culture has its own weapons and its own knives and spoons, and each knife and spoon has a whole story to it.

Season Four started with a pretty complicated environment in Mon Cala, a water world. Did that represent a benchmark at the time?
The complication of Mon Cala was how much there was to build in one episode. We had to build an entire civilization. That was a strain on the production, because we had none of it. We didn't have any of the buildings, we didn't have any of the coral elements. It all had to be created from scratch. When you're doing that, you have the same amount of time to create an episode whether you're creating a whole civilization or just the Jedi Temple. So that was very taxing.

The most complex environment still for that season was Wasskah, where Chewbacca was, at the end of Season Three. That was a groundbreaking episode where we looked at the environment and said, "Every episode now has to be as detailed as this one." In Season Four, the environments that were organic were becoming much more lush.

Bo-Katan was first seen in the episode, "A Friend in Need." How did that story come about?
I like that episode very much. I had to fight for that episode. I wanted very badly in this season to have a Mandalorian story arc. I knew that people really liked Death Watch in Season Two, and people were interested in what was going on there.

In the original Season Four story conference, I presented an outline that didn't end up being used. But what happened was another story, a planned four-parter, ended up being three parts, so we had an extra story. George said, "Well, let's do Filoni's Death Watch story." To George's credit, he really came up with it. I was pitching a story that was more centered around Satine and possible things for her future, but George definitely wanted Ahsoka and Lux in the story. When he fleshed that out and we worked on it in the room, I thought it was really interesting; it moves forward Ahsoka's possible would-be relationship with Lux.

1/

1 / Dave Filoni poses with a Phase I clone trooper helmet for the character Commander Wolffe. Filoni personally designed the next version of Wolffe's helmet, choosing the visor shape specifically because it worked well with the wolf emblem.

2 / A dramatic sketch of the bounty hunter Embo as illustrated by Dave Filoni.

3 /   4 /

3 / Filoni's art depicting
Bo-Katan Kryze.

4 / The writers of The
Clone Wars advocated
killing off Maul at the
end of the series. But
George Lucas vetoed
this idea, leaving
Savage Opress on the
chopping block.

5 / The design of the
Phase II clone trooper
helmet evokes the
stormtrooper helmets
seen in the first *Star
Wars* movie, *A New
Hope* (1977).

6 / Ahsoka Tano would
prove to be one of
the shows biggest
surprises as she
rapidly become one
of the saga's most
beloved characters.

I also wanted to show a dynamic change in Death Watch. George wanted them to be more like a biker gang and more violent, which really allowed them to shine in a different light, and it gave me the opportunity to add a female Mandalorian to the screen. That was its own whole process of designing the helmets and bringing actor Katee Sackhoff on. It introduced a lot of new elements, and I knew that I wanted to direct it. I like to control Ahsoka's destiny very directly at times.

A lot happened during Season Five, things like the deaths of Duchess Satine Kryze and Savage Opress, Maul versus Darth Sidious, and the trials and tribulations of Ahsoka Tano. Was this all planned to lead up to this point?
I think it all just happened naturally, to be honest. I don't know that there ultimately was a plan to say, "This year we're going to kill a bunch of main characters," (laughs). It's just that as the story evolves, it demands it after a while. You can't have certain characters around in the future (of the saga), so you have to deal with them. It's more a natural progression. We had been asking a lot of questions by creating these situations, and it was time to answer those questions.

George Lucas was heavily involved in the story creation of the show. Did he have any specific instructions for the season?
The origin of the idea, Maul will face Darth Sidious, was a George idea, "I want them to fight." When it came down to the directing of where they were going to fight, the staging of the fight, that's what I brought to the table. So we went over the broad story beats, and then he trusted me and the writers, and the rest of the team, to bring it to the screen. That freedom and trust from him is what in some ways made the show. We were developing more and experimenting more, and all the results are part of that collaboration.

Is there anything he resisted that you had to push for?
I don't know about "resisted," because when George doesn't want something to happen, it's probably not going to happen (laughs). The idea for Savage to revert back to his natural form, we came up with that stuff on the fly. Everything that I did creatively was really based on the initial discussions that I had with George, and taking tons of notes and making visual drawing notes. If you look at the original drawings that I did in the writers' room on the day, they're very close to what ended up visually on-screen.

5 /

Five Reasons To Love
Star Wars: The Clone Wars

- It gave us the most *Star Wars* stories from George Lucas. Most people know that George Lucas created *The Clone Wars* series and is its executive producer. But not everyone realizes that many, many stories, nearly all of them, from the series' original run come straight either from Lucas or were molded by his personal input, often re-shaped in the editing suite. With 121 episodes, more than 40 hours of *Star Wars* tales from the guy who started it all.

- It introduced Ahsoka Tano. One of *The Clone Wars*' biggest surprises was that Anakin Skywalker had a Padawan—Ahsoka Tano—and that their relationship would form the heart of the series. Much like her master, Ahsoka starts out brash and fallible, at one point even losing her lightsaber; but over the course of the series she matures, becoming a true Jedi. Today, Ahsoka (voiced by Ashley Eckstein), the first on-screen lead female Jedi, stands with *Star Wars*' most beloved characters.

Continues on page 115

6 /

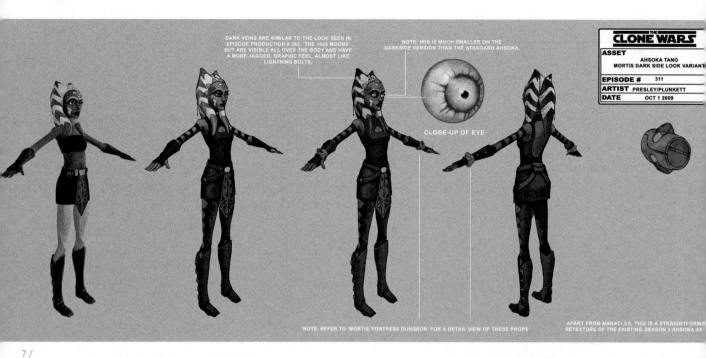

DARK VEINS ARE SIMILAR TO THE LOOK SEEN IN EPISODE PRODUCTION # 202, 'THE 1000 MOONS' BUT ARE VISIBLE ALL OVER THE BODY AND HAVE A MORE JAGGED, GRAPHIC FEEL, ALMOST LIKE LIGHTNING BOLTS.

NOTE: IRIS IS MUCH SMALLER ON THE DARKSIDE VERSION THAN THE STANDARD AHSOKA.

CLOSE-UP OF EYE

CLONE WARS	
ASSET	AHSOKA TANO MORTIS DARK SIDE LOOK VARIANT
EPISODE #	311
ARTIST	PRESLEY/PLUNKETT
DATE	OCT 1 2009

NOTE: REFER TO 'MORTIS FORTRESS DUNGEON' FOR A DETAIL VIEW OF THESE PROPS

APART FROM MANACLES, THIS IS A STRAIGHTFORWA RETEXTURE OF THE EXISTING SEASON 3 AHSOKA AS

7 /

7 / Unlike the older characters of *The Clone Wars*, the audience can sense the passage of time during the series by watching Ahsoka Tano grow closer to adulthood.

8 / Though Ahsoka's original lightsaber blades were green, Anakin Skywalker adapted the crystals to emit a blue color in Season 7.

9 / This concept art of young Ahsoka Tano meeting Jedi Master Plo Kloon was drawn by Dave Filoni, who was supervising director at the time.

10 / While character development is vital to the show, *The Clone Wars* doesn't avoid showing epic space battles!

The main thing is that I couldn't really change the stories. They are what they are. We're going have a younglings story arc, and we're going to have a droids story arc, and then we're going to behead people with Maul (laughs). What I tried to do was to make it all feel very much like *Star Wars*. For the Maul stuff, we were very much going for *Revenge of the Sith*. When you subdivide the *Star Wars* films, you see that they are as varied in tone and attitude as our episodic series. But it all naturally flowed together.

You had a major role in creating and developing characters like the pirate Hondo Ohnaka and Ahsoka Tano, and they get to live on, they're still out there in the *Star Wars* galaxy.
I don't think of my role in the creation of the characters much, because the characters, they just seem like they were always there in the *Star Wars* galaxy and I was lucky to be the one to relay their stories to the audience. I'm always excited when other creative people want to use those characters, and I'm always very thankful when they approach me about it, so that I can help them and say, "Well, this is what we intended and these were our plans. I'd appreciate it if you would follow these ideas because these are things George Lucas and I worked out." That's still very important.

The last story arc of the season feels like a finale. How do you feel about it as an ending?
I had a decent inkling that it would be the end of the show on Cartoon Network. You look at it realistically, the show had been on the air for five years. That's a long time for an animated show that's not in prime time. So I thought, if this is the last season on Cartoon

Network, then I want to have a proper ending for the people who have watched it. That was the whole thing behind giving Ahsoka some finality in that timeline. It was an important moment. I directed that as if it were this big goodbye, knowing that it might be a goodbye to at least the way *The Clone Wars* was broadcast, if not the show itself. And I'm happy with that. I was very glad that it ended with Ahsoka, because it very much began with Ahsoka in *The Clone Wars* movie. Everyone pointed out from the beginning—we know what happens to Anakin, we know what happens to Obi-Wan, and to Padmé, so where's the mystery and where's the suspense? While every episode definitely was not about her, Ahsoka's story thread shows you the way the Jedi are looked at in the war, how they're fighting the war, what they're questioning. It's an ending of one large phase for that character, which is, "What does it mean for me to be in the Clone Wars and what's my role?" Ultimately she chooses a different path than the Jedi do, or the Republic chooses. So she's now on a third strand. She doesn't become a part of the Empire, though I don't think Ahsoka would consider herself a Jedi in the post-Republic era. It turned out that *The Clone Wars* was largely about this girl, Ahsoka.

When you look back on *The Clone Wars*, what does it mean to you as a body of work?
I think that by the end of Season Five we definitely were getting it right. We had a lot to learn in the beginning, and I think that we made certain mistakes that are unavoidable. When you're a fan, you do things that you've seen in the movies repeatedly, and you want to capture that feeling so you're repeating things more than innovating.

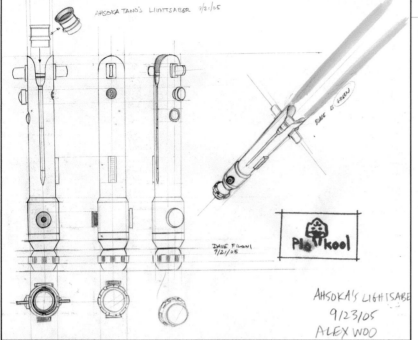

8 /

AHSOKA TANO'S LIGHTSABER 9/21/05

BLADE IS GREEN

DAVE FILONI
9/21/05

Plaкool

AHSOKA'S LIGHTSABER
9/23/05
ALEX WOO

9 /

Continues from page 113

- It explored Mandalorian culture, something fans had longed to see. Without *The Clone Wars*' world-building, we might not have *The Mandalorian* series. Indeed, even its executive producer Jon Favreau took his first steps into a galaxy far, far away as the voice of Pre Vizsla, a militant Mandalorian who was in league with—and then battled—Maul.

- It deepened our understanding of Anakin Skywalker. The prequels showed us Anakin Skywalker at different stages of his life, but with *The Clone Wars*, Lucas went deeper, illustrating how the young and impatient Padawan of *Attack of the Clones* becomes the confident but flawed warrior seen of *Revenge of the Sith*. We see how becoming a mentor helps him grow; how he and Obi-Wan Kenobi are an amazing team; and just how good, creative, and caring a person he was.

- It revealed new aspects of Force lore. Mortis. Moraband. Force Priestesses. Lucas revealed more about the mysteries of the Force in *The Clone Wars* than ever before, while still leaving much to the imagination. The central episodes, popularly known as "The Mortis Trilogy" from Season Three and "The Yoda Arc" from Season 6, *The Lost Missions*, are thrilling, frightening, and magical. They will change the way you look at that mystical energy field and its role in the saga.

10 /

11 /

11 / Dave Filoni directed the episode "Padawan Lost," in which a kidnapped Ahsoka takes refuge with other lost Jedi apprentices. Art by David Le Merrer.

12 / Ahsoka Tano's space suit first appeared in the episode "Cargo of Doom," and was designed to keep her recognizable uniform elements visible.

George warned us in the beginning. We didn't quite understand what he was talking about, but as we went along we became better at what we were doing. I can't separate the stories we told from the people that made them. It was a great experience, and I tried to make it a good experience for the crew working on it, because we were working very hard. For me personally, it was the greatest education in filmmaking I could ever get—all because of George and his patience when teaching me, being a mentor, not getting frustrated when I wasn't really getting it right. Just taking the time to teach all of us how to do this the way that he did it, and at times, I hope, to

get close to that effervescent magic that is *Star Wars*. To take the things he taught me and move forward with them. He would come to us with ideas, and we would sit down and hash them out, and then we would go to work making these stories. He left a lot of the critical decisions to me, but I always had to keep in mind what he was after, what he had taught me. It was awesome to have him come back to the theater and sit down and watch them. It was awesome and it was nerve-wracking and it was exciting. So I owe George very much. Everything that I do going forward with my career, I think, will be a reflection of that knowledge that I gained from him. I take it

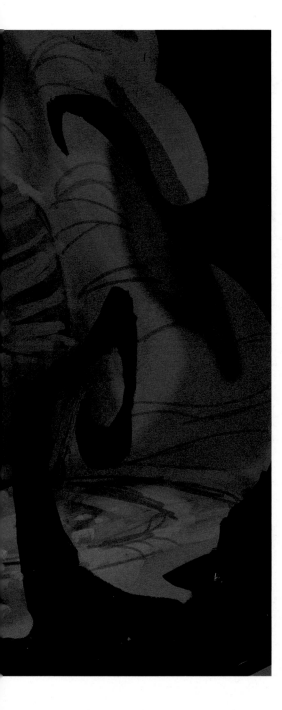

SPACESUIT
MINUS
HELMET

seriously, that it's part of a legacy. It's a privilege, and an incredibly lucky, lucky thing that I became a part of. The people who have luck know that a lot of hard work goes into getting yourself into the position to experience that luck. A lot of different things had to come together for a lot of different people to make this show work. But the foundation of it all definitely was George Lucas and his belief in us as a group, and his willingness to teach us and guide us and let us make *Star Wars*, with him and then for him in the later years of *Clone Wars*. I think that, for him, it was a rewarding experience, as well—that he had a team of people dedicated to making *Star Wars* the way that he wanted it.

1 /

2 /

DARREN MARSHALL
CHARACTER DESIGN & MAQUETTE SCULPTOR

How did you come to work on *Star Wars: The Clone Wars*?
I was already here as part of Industrial Light & Magic [ILM]. Dave Filoni [*The Clone Wars* supervising director] saw some of my older maquettes and asked if I could join his team to realize some of the main characters.

What does the job entail?
Dave always likes me to sculpt important characters and the classic characters. He likes me to block out a maquette and to stylize it into the style of our show, to see what it's going to look like in 3D.
For me, it's easier to block a figure out in clay, because I come from a stop-motion background. I worked for many years at a place called Mackinnon & Saunders in Manchester, England, which makes puppets for TV commercials and feature films.

Which was the first character you built for the show?
It was Count Dooku. That was the very first thing we started with back in 2005. It was just a head maquette. His look was very extreme…as it still is.

Tarkin made his debut on *The Clone Wars* during Season 3. Is it fun to play with those established actors' features and exaggerate them?
It's great fun! That was one of my favorite characters to do. I grew up with all the Hammer films—which featured Peter Cushing and Christopher Lee—so that was a major one for me.

I love the British bad guys in *Star Wars*, and both actors have great, expressive faces that work well for our show.

Your work was presented to George Lucas in the initial pitch for the show. What was his reaction and what notes did he supply?
They showed him the original maquettes that I built. Originally we did full figures of Anakin, Obi-Wan, and Ahsoka. The production team experimented with extreme lighting, and they took some photographs to see how the stylized features of faces would work under different lighting conditions. George responded really well to the maquettes and the pitch—which was great for us, because I was really nervous.

1/ Padmé Amidala in maquette form.
2/ Darren Marshall works on the Ahsoka Tano maquette.
3/ Clawdite bounty hunter, Cato Parasitti.

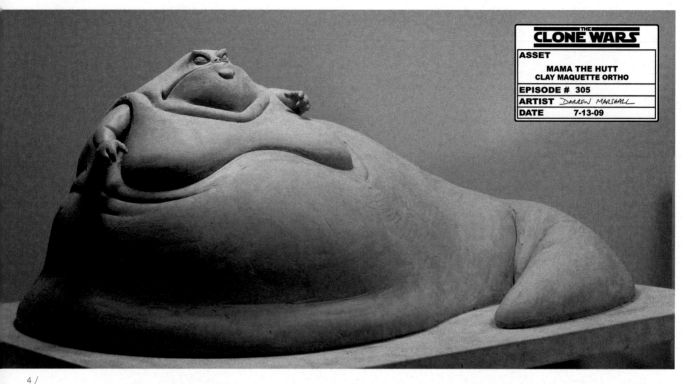

CLONE WARS

ASSET	**MAMA THE HUTT CLAY MAQUETTE ORTHO**
EPISODE #	305
ARTIST	Darren Marshall
DATE	7-13-09

4 /

4 / Mama the Hutt who made her only appearance in the Season 3 episode, "Hunt for Ziro."

5 / A stylized Palpatine sculpture.

6 / A Rodian formed of clay.

7 / Jedi Master Eeth Koth made his *Star Wars: The Clone Wars* debut in the episode "Grievous Intrigue."

8 / Klatooinian bounty hunter Castas, from Season 2 episode, "R2 Come Home."

Dave was in that meeting with George and I remember him coming out and being really excited by the reaction he got. That was a great sign for us.

What materials do you use?
It's specialized professional clay called Chavant. I used to use traditional Plasticine, which was a lot softer. They had some Chavant clay left over from the feature films, so they gave me some. It was quite firm and you could get those sharp, stylized angles for the facial features.

How long does it take to build each piece?
I'll read a script, and then I'll block out a head in a day or two. I'll take a photograph of the head if Dave's approved it, and then I'll put it into Photoshop on my computer. Next I'll draw a body and costume, and then paint the whole thing over the top of the pictures of the maquette head and the body for the finished design. Chewbacca took a fair bit longer because of the accuracy we were trying to go for on the fur.

Was it a daunting prospect to recreate him?
It was, because he's so recognizable, and all the fans are going to be scrutinizing him! There was a huge amount of pressure to get Chewie right. We don't do realistic hair on the show, so we had to come up with a way of stylizing the fur. We went to the Lucasfilm Archives, where they had one of the old Chewbacca masks that had been used in *Return of the Jedi*. It was very old and crumbling at the front. They also had the *Revenge of the Sith* prequel costume. We noticed that the prequel fur was very straight and

soft, but the original costume used yak fur, which had an extremely wavy shag to it. We responded to that because we thought we could stylize that better. The look of the character in *The Clone Wars* was based on *A New Hope* and *The Empire Strikes Back*, because of that yak fur. It's very scrappy looking. It's like one of those old 1970s rugs that your aunt used to have in her living room.

Which do you prefer working on, human characters or aliens?
I like them both. I'm in my 40s now and the original Star Wars came out when I was seven, so I love the original trilogy. I usually get the classic characters to work on: I've been given Bossk, Greedo, a Gamorrean Guard and Grand Moff Tarkin. Tarkin and Chewbacca were big, so I really wanted to try and get them as accurate as possible while keeping true to the style of our show.

How much artistic license do you have when you're working?
If you're doing a classic character, you can't really change it. The only way you're changing it is by putting a style mark on it, such as Bossk or Greedo. It's taking those very "creature-y" textures and doing a new angle on the features, but still trying to make it look like the characters. For Chewie, there were so many great reference photographs that I hadn't seen before, that I could try to get every detail.

For example, he's got a slight under-bite in some of the photographs, and I tried to put that in the maquette. Hopefully the fans can look at it and instantly know that's Chewie!

5 /

6/

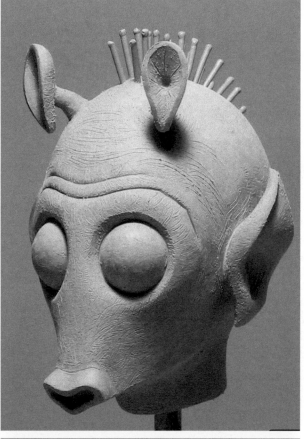

7 /

8 /

JOEL ARON
CG LIGHTING & EFFECTS SUPERVISOR

1 / Flametroopers take down the Geonosians.

2 / Joel Aron's psychedelic lighting.

3 / Kamino, previously seen in *Star Wars: Attack of the Clones*, revisted with Aron taking the challenge of depicting water in animation.

What does a CG lighting and effects supervisor do?
It's a job that was unique to *Star Wars: The Clone Wars*. A CG supervisor is the nerd on the show that knows how all the strings are tied together in order to keep it running. The role encompasses lighting and effects, and I've done lighting almost my entire career, and I've done effects my entire career, so it kind of blended together! The lighting part of the job is making each episode look the way that we want it to look. For the effects, I have to make sure we're not making the show too photo-realistic, and that we're putting style into it.

What is the difference between doing the effects for live action and working on a CG show like *The Clone Wars*?
I went through a learning curve when I first got onto the show. I worked on feature films at ILM for a little over 17 years before coming here. I knew how

to do photo-real graphics, and that was it. Working with live-action, especially working at ILM for that entire time, you strive to make effects so believable, that you don't question that it's an effect. Working at that caliber you get yourself stuck into the groove of "no style." There's not going to be any graphic enhancement or anything that you can do stylistically to make the effects look better.

Coming onto *The Clone Wars*, I was sent to Singapore to work with the effects team there. At the time there were just three guys. Two of them, who were new to effects, said, "We want to make our explosions look better." So I said, "Okay, let's get to the bottom of this, and we'll figure it out." I brought a bunch of tools that ILM no longer used to do effects and started doing these explosions. I sent these explosions back to Skywalker Ranch to see what they thought, and the first comment I got was, "Too photo-real." So I went back to the drawing board and tried to figure it out again.

Almost half a year later, when I'd become a full-on member on the production, Dave Filoni [*The Clone Wars*' Supervising Director] came to me and said, "I want to do these rooster tails behind these speeders, but I don't want to do the usual cloud of dust and debris that kicks up behind a speeder when it flies, I want to do something stylistically like anime."

So Dave dropped a Japanese anime show called *Wolf's Rain* (2003) in front of me, and I watched what the snow looked like and what the rooster tails did behind cars that were speeding down the road, and it looked like a saw tooth pattern. I thought, *Okay, I really need to think creatively here and draw on my roots of understanding fine art.* I'm a huge impressionist fan, and I thought, *Well let's just make this look impressionistic.* So I painted what the effects would look like, and made my painting come to life, and it was at that point that I realized I had finally broken through the barrier of live-action into stylized effects that we do on the show.

You really need to take everything you learned from live-action and use small parts of it, but don't use the final look.

What's the secret of a good explosion?
An explosion is made up of a pop-flash, then you've got the big boom. The secret is beats; you need to have the beats.

If you just have a big boom, the sound guys go and do a big boom and that's it. So you get this big push with the destruction that's happening. Then you have the fireball flash, the fire comes up and will quickly go to smoke. It's all really quick, but in order to have that beat, stylistically you need a follow-up, what I would call a concussion. You have the big boom and then you rush air or dust at the camera, like in a ring, and that's the second event.

Now, those two events are what make up every single explosion you see in live-action, so we've taken the first initial boom, and we've drawn in anime spikes, too. So when you watch these explosions, for about three or four frames, you'll see what appear to be hand drawn spikes, which is exactly what they are! Those spikes are actually just flat texture, and there's a few of them that are rotated so they don't look flat when combined. After that, we have the spikes just completely disappear, and then there's a shockwave: a rush of air that comes towards the camera.

The final event is what I call "shark bits," and I refer to this all the time with the explosions, because it is a throwback to my favorite movie, *Jaws* (1975). One of my all-time favorite elements of *Jaws* is when they blow up the shark at the end of the movie. There are bits of exploded shark that continue to fall down while Brody is in the water laughing, so I always have shark bits when I do an explosion. That's the third beat of the explosion. You have the boom, the rush, and the bits falling down. The nice thing is you can use any one of those elements separately off the screen to give the sound guys even more to work with so you don't need to do the whole effect. Sometimes you can just have shark bits falling down, and the sound guys will go, "Oh, there must have been an explosion off-screen." Or you'll see a rush of air go by and then shark bits. So those are my three elements, the three beats, and layering up each one of them is the key to making it all work together.

After mastering fire and explosions, what was the next big challenge?
Water. Water is maddening, as is trying to render fire. I would equate trying to get water to do what you want to do in CG as repainting a white room, because you don't know where you started, you don't know where you've ended, you don't know what's dry, you don't know what's wet. It all disappears, and you start to lose your mind a little bit!

When I found out that we go to Kamino in Season Three, and that we were going to be doing water, I knew I had tried it before on "Children of the Force" in Season Two. For that, I painted the water and put it on a flat surface, and made that surface look like waves. Around the same time, United Airlines had this weird hand-drawn commercial, with this water that was a whole bunch of repeated patterns. I took that as my cue to say, "You know what? As long as it acts like water, we can make it look like whatever we want."

I worked with this artist, Sang Lee, who painted the base color of the ocean to just be a bunch of brushstrokes that are dark and green and blue, and that kind of hue, and he painted stylistically what looked like the foam on top of the water, and that's all we did. Then we put a little bit of atmospheric haze blowing by, a little bit of mist rolling on the surface, to complete the effect.

Which episodes would you say have really raised the bar in Season Two?
"Landing at Point Rain" was a huge leap forward in terms of what we were able to do for effects on the show. The Zillo Beast episodes were groundbreaking in that we started destroying things. We'd never been able to physically destroy anything on the show before.

"Lethal Trackdown" was another epic challenge to pull off creatively, for the lighting and the effects. Dave would constantly come into my office and talk about it, because everything had to be better than just a cardboard-looking set. For that episode and "R2 Come Home" we really tried to push it to the next level.

The biggest leap, however, was the Boba Fett trilogy. We were able to make the environments so rich. We totally changed the whole look of the show, and really made the environments something the characters actually had to wrestle with. Everything

4 /

4 / Plo Koon and Ahsoka under the lights inspired by a Turkish bar in "Lethal Trackdown."

5 / The Zillo Beast brings destruction to *The Clone Wars*!

6 / A scene from "Landing at Point Rain," an episode that marked a progression in what Aron and the team could do regarding effects on the show.

to me is light: light balance, light ratio, proper composition of shape, color, and balance in every single shot. Dave and I are both huge Caravaggio fans. I'm a photographer and so I love any painting with light.

I also love *National Geographic*, and for "Lethal Trackdown" I stumbled upon an article about Turkey, with a beautiful picture of this bar that I loved. I showed Dave and he said, "Sure, just try it out to see what it looks like." I was also influenced by the Zeitgeist bar in San Francisco. I was inspired by the back room where they have these fuzzy velvet couches. The most beautiful place I've been inspired by is 18th Century Paris. I had just seen the movie *Chéri* (2009) and said, "Dave, I want this planet to be like 18th Century Paris!"

5 /

6 /

KEITH KELLOGG

ANIMATION SUPERVISOR

Can you describe the role of Animation Supervisor and what the job entails?
We had three studios working for us, so basically every studio submitted their shots to me on a daily basis. We were working on multiple episodes at any given time, and I reviewed these shots—around 80 to 100 of them each day—and made notes on them. There were also many times where I recorded myself, as sometimes that was the easiest way to get across my thoughts on the performance.

There was also a lot of work that is done upfront, earlier in the design process of the episode. From the start of the show, the assets were created. These were modeled, both in-house and overseas from the amazing designs on the show. I would give feedback on these and make sure that the characters can move properly. We also had rigging dailies to take a look at the upcoming characters in the episodes.

This was to make sure that they meet the deformation and motion requirements that are necessary for the show. Sometimes a still image can look good, but we have some really crazy designs and outfits—plus the armor of the clone troopers—so you have to make sure that it all works onscreen.

What were the biggest challenges you faced on the show?
With every episode we were creating new characters, new locations, and new designs—so each and every show had its own special set of challenges. Obviously, we had our main characters: Anakin, Ahsoka, Obi-Wan and so on, but with different story arcs we also got to delve into other characters that people haven't seen in the *Star Wars* universe yet. It's a lot of work creating those characters on an episodic basis, and making sure the character stays consistent across our three studios.

1 / Anakin faces Count Dooku in battle.

2 / Kellogg had the challenge of making the identical army of clones distinct.

3 / C-3PO was just one of many returning characters.

4 / Keith Kellogg. Photograph by Joel Aron.

4 /

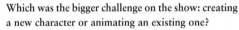

2 /

3 /

Which was the bigger challenge on the show: creating a new character or animating an existing one?
To me, it's creating a new character. Occasionally, due to different production and scheduling things, we had different studios animate a new character. That's a big challenge, because there's a lot of different ways to animate a character.

A really great example of that was Pong Krell in the Umbara quadrilogy. He was created across two different studios, with each doing two episodes. A lot of my job was trying to make sure that we maintain a complete character with all of the subtle characteristics intact.

Was it difficult to make sure all the clones in the show were different?
The key was finding their different personalities. The arc on Umbara is mainly about clones. Obviously, they all look the same, so trying to make sure the audience could tell them apart by both their body language and facial expressions was a big challenge. Some clones would be more questioning, so I'd have their inner eyebrows up just a little bit, just to kind of get that subtle nuance across that this is the one that's questioning the orders. There might have been another who is angry about what's going on, so maybe his brows were down a bit more, his lower lids up slightly more; just subtle little things like that.

Do you have a favorite character?
I tend to like the villains, just because they can really chew up scenery; you can be a little more aggressive with them, have little jaw-rolls here and there and little nuances in the face. It might be a facial tic like we had with Osi Sobeck in "The Citadel." Whenever he spoke to Count Dooku, we gave him a little bit of an eye-twitch to show how nervous he was. With villains, you can push them probably about 20 percent more than what you can do with your heroes.

How did you approach bringing Chewbacca into *The Clone Wars*?

When we introduced Chewbacca to the show, it was the first time the world had ever seen Chewbacca being performed by somebody else. [Original Chewbacca actor] Peter Mayhew was really heavily involved in our recreation of the character and he gave us subtle ideas of how Chewbacca should behave. Peter is the only person to have ever portrayed Chewbacca, and we tried to make sure we were true to his vision. We made sure we incorporated the fact he's not as aggressive as some of the other Wookiees, and he's a little more curious, and that he has the movie-Chewbacca's little bow-leggedness. Hearing all that from Peter's perspective helped us to bring that character to life.

There was also a technological advancement because we had moving fur for the first time. Chewbacca was an incredibly heavy character to animate; the animators struggled a bit at first, because of how dense he was, but we came up with ways we could help with that.

Did you enjoy working with some of the guest directors?

There were some really big names, for sure. Duwayne Dunham's episode was an incredibly challenging thing to do because we were going underwater for a three-episode arc. We had to create all-new environments and the characters had to be constantly treading water and moving. I chose a lot of the underwater fight scenes from the James Bond movie *Thunderball*

(1965), as reference for the animation studios to look at, and I'd constantly be sending them clips of other things. Reference is always the key.

Another guest director was Walter Murch, who worked on the Umbara arc. Everybody around the studio was obviously really happy he was here and learned a great deal from him. He's got so much experience. You can really see his camera-work and all the details in the Umbara arc; you feel like you're down in the actual trenches, fighting alongside the clones.

How closely did you work with the voice actors?

One thing I've always found to be a really big help in animation is filming the actual ADR [Additional Dialogue Recording] sessions of the actors. You can see what the actors were thinking and get an idea of what their emotions were when they recorded the scenes. In studying the performance, you always find little things that you can bring out that take the performance to another level.

Some of our animators don't actually speak English, and it's a real challenge for them to animate lip-sync. So to actually be able to show when the mouth is opening and closing, and what the different shapes are, helps them a great deal.

Would you say that the animation is stylized or is it striving to be more real?

It's a stylized realism. We're definitely more realistic than a lot of animated shows are, but we do still have a specific style that we're trying to hit. We have a very

6 /

5 / Kellogg had a great deal of input into realizing Jedi Master Pong Krell.

6 / The clones in action on Umbara.

7/ Ahsoka and Tarkin, a legacy character who made his mark on *The Clone Wars*.

8 / The action goes beneath the surface of Mon Cala.

7 / angular kind of design and I tried to emphasize that angularity a little bit. Making sure that we have really strong poses is a big deal, especially when lightsabers are blocking blasters. We definitely are stylized, but there is also a high level of realism.

What was your biggest goal on the show in terms of bringing realism to the animation?

In any animated show, sometimes there can be little things which draw you out of the story—for instance, if a walk looks a little stilted or you suddenly realize that something doesn't look quite right. My biggest goal was to make sure that none of those things appeared on-screen. The second task I wanted to accomplish was really pushing both the facial performances as well as the acting in order to bring a new level of animation to *The Clone Wars*.

8 / Also, we have so many different kinds of characters and a lot of them walked the same and did similar things, so, later on in the season, we introduced a different species with a little bit of a different walk and different gait and tried to give them some personality through that.

ROB COLEMAN

ANIMATION CONSULTANT

What are the day-to-day challenges of an animation consultant?

Dave Filoni, the series' supervising director, and Catherine Winder, our launch producer, had both worked in animation before but had not worked in the *Star Wars* universe. George Lucas asked me to meet with them and immerse them in the world of *Star Wars*. The role of animation consultant came out of that early working relationship with Dave Filoni.

Dave is a very talented storyboard artist, and he'd come from doing the 2D animated *Avatar: The Last Airbender*, but he'd not worked in computer graphics before, and he'd not worked with *Star Wars* characters. He is a huge *Star Wars* fan, as the world now knows, but we crafted the role of animation consultant so that I would be able to give input, and critique all animation coming in from our overseas studios. The day to day work was to review the animation and give feedback on the performances. I also worked with Dave to find the right balance of time spent on the animation. For me, that first year, 2005, was tough. We were trying to find the right movement for these characters. George talked about a stylized East-meets-West anime influence

but animated for a North American audience. As an animation consultant, I worked very closely with Dave to craft what that ultimately ended up being the look.

How did you make sure the show felt like *Star Wars*?
George Lucas was very involved and he was extremely involved in the early days, working with Dave Filoni, the writers, and the various episodic directors in describing to us what he was looking for. I was always coaching directors to go and look at the original *Star Wars* movie, so they had an idea of the kind of framing and cutting that George likes. What Dave and Henry Gilroy (writer) tried to do in the early days was to recapture that 1977 feel, so—and this is the fun part— there was a lot of homework going back and looking at the old movies and really studying them from a stylistic and directing-choice point of view. We looked at camera choices, cutting choices. George uses a certain kind of lens and there is a certain kind of cutting that he does. Once you become

well-versed in that, you can make him very happy. I'd worked side by side with him for so many years that I had an advantage over the other episodic directors. I already knew how to communicate with George. I was very fluent in George Lucas, let's put it that way! This is Dave Filoni's show. Being asked to be the animation consultant and directing some episodes helped to move the series along. I went over and taught classes in Singapore. I ended up doing the "Downfall of a Droid" and "Duel of the Droids" episodes, which were the very first two shows to come out of Singapore. They wanted me to help shepherd them along, which I was happy to do. They are probably the roughest shows that we did, because they were the first two out of the gate. I've directed three more since then and they are much stronger because the team had more experience and more familiarity with the characters and the cameras than they did in those two episodes.

1 / The main characters as seen during *Star Wars: The Clone Wars'* first season.

2 / Rob Coleman.

3 /

3 / Ahsoka faces General Grievous in "Duel of the Droids."

4 / Grievous and Gha Nachkt examine R2-D2.

5 / R2 in trouble!

6 / R2 battles R3-S6

7 / R2 proves his tough guy credentials in an epic fight.

Is there anything you would change about them?
The hardest thing to do as a director is to say, "That's good enough." If you don't start approving work, and you don't have a vision of what you want the show to look like, it will never be finished! I think where I was successful with George was that I was always able to step into the river and say, "That's good enough." The river keeps flowing past you, and you'll see better work coming later on, but you have to stick with what you did before. There are certainly shots in those episodes that I would love to have back, but I don't regret it because we had to deliver the show. The show is animated in about a fifth of the time of a feature film, so we didn't get the subtlety and fidelity in the faces and lip-synching in those earlier shows. Later episodes are far better, because I was able to spend time and really hone the team's awareness of what was important in the face. In those earlier episodes it was all hands on deck!

How is an episode put together?
Dave Filoni is the supervising director. He works directly with George Lucas and the writers to create an overall plan for all of the episodes each season. He's there at the beginning with the producer. It usually takes a couple of days to a week, and they plan out in very rough form what will happen.

They come up with episode synopses which are about a paragraph long for each episode, and describe what happens to the heroes, what the problems are, and what gets solved.

The writing team divides up the episodes between them and they start writing. Once the first drafts come in, Dave and George read them and make notes and decisions. Then they start choosing episodes that are actually going to be made. That's when an episodic director gets involved. They'd call the director in and say, "Rob we've got an R2-D2 show coming up"—in my case it was a two parter—"and here's an early draft."

The director gives notes, as a fresh pair of eyes to the story. Then, in maybe a few days or a week, a shooting draft is ready. At that point, the episodic director works with the story-board artists, doing storyboards on paper or computer, or in my case going straight to 3D computer graphics to map out what the scenes are going to look like. You spend maybe six weeks mapping out the whole show, so you have a version of the show done in storyboards or in computer animatics that describes visually what the show's going to look like.

There might be a still image of Anakin standing, and I would record people in the studio for temp dialogue and work with editor Jason Tucker to cut it all together, so it's to length, but nothing's animated at that stage, and nothing's got color. It's usually just black and white

6 /

7 /

or gray. I'd present that to George, and then he would give me notes. I'd do a revision on that and present it for a final look. Then George would sign off on it.

As an episodic director you "package up the show." This means you make shot-by-shot directing notes on what you want to see happening. You might say Anakin walks onto the bridge of the Twilight. Ahsoka's sitting there with Artoo, and turns to him and says the line. You give director points, like "Anakin's angry at this point because he's just come from such-and-such a place and he's irritated by this or that." When the animators get it in Singapore they understand, because otherwise it could be animated completely out of context. Animators might get five shots in a row, but they may not know what's come before so it's very important as a director that you tell them. Normally, an episodic director would then leave that process and go onto the next show, but I then critiqued, not only the animation coming in for my show, but also for the other four episodic directors.

What are your favorite scenes from the show?

I really like the writing on those shows, and to be able to see Artoo becoming a tougher little guy was a lot of fun for me. I would say the scene with him fighting with the other droid was a favorite. It was fun to figure out how to shoot that and what was going to

happen there. The writers had outlined the entire fight, but as a director you get to pick all the angles, which was fun. The assassin droids coming to life in the hold of the ship was really fun to direct, and to invent how we saw the IG-88s jumping around. We'd only ever seen them standing still in *The Empire Strikes Back*, so to get them to jump and leap and spin their heads around was a highlight for me.

I was trying to go with the opposite of what the character looked like. If you have a toy or you saw it in the movies, he's just standing there not doing anything. He just looks so rigid, and I thought from an animator's point of view "Let's take that rigidity and just throw it away!" Let's really surprise the fans, so that when these things leap up they're actually much more flexible than their "Tin Man" appearance would allude to. What I was able to do is make it into a vertical fight.

I didn't want to just have a fight on the ground; we've seen that so many times. I had this set that had been already outlined in the script where it was described as this big warehouse with shelves upon shelves of droid parts. I went up to the Home Depot store and walked around the aisles. I was thinking, "Wouldn't it be cool to look up and see those droids jumping and leaping from side to side?" So that's how that started. I thought that was just a neat image.

1 /

NOTES FROM THE FRONTLINE

Walter Murch redefined the role of the cinematic sound editor/mixer, coining the term "sound designer" for *Apocalypse Now* (1979), a title foreshadowed by his "sound montage" credit for *The Conversation* (1974). Murch later turned his hand to directing, helming *Return to Oz*, the 1985 sequel to the beloved classic. It was his friend George Lucas who offered Murch the opportunity to take the director's chair once again for *The Clone Wars* Season Four episode of the Umbaran quadrilogy, "The General."

How did you first get invited to direct an episode of *The Clone Wars*?
I heard George Lucas had asked a friend of mine, Bob Dalva, who's a film editor, director, and cameraman, to be a guest director on the show (Season 2's "The Deserter"), and I kept tabs on him, checking how it was going. He was having a great time doing it. I think it was a year later that George said, "What about you? Do you want to be a guest director?"

Did you choose a script?
They just said here it is. I would've been overwhelmed if I had to choose, because I didn't know anything about the process other than what Bob and George had told me. It was much better just to get an assignment.

What did George tell you about the show?
Not much. He said, "It's great, you'll love it!" What he's interested in with guest directors is people coming on board and injecting whatever it is that makes a metal into an alloy: a little extra something that's not normally in the metal, but that helps to turn it into

something else – iron into steel, brass into bronze, hopefully stronger. There are four directors on staff, very talented directors, who are each working on three projects at once in various stages, whereas a guest director is only working on one thing and doesn't hang around after the job is done. I wasn't involved at all in the final animation. It's just a very specific 12-week gig.

So you had 12 weeks. At this point was the script already written?
Yes, it was finished and, other than meeting at the end of the process, I never had any interaction with the writer. Dave Filoni did ask, "What do you think about the script? Any ideas?" In this story, the two clones, Fives and Hardcase, have to penetrate an alien airbase and there's a perimeter fence around it. In the original script, they walked up to the fence and turned it off with some device they had. I thought we should make it a little harder, just to get a bit

more action into it. So the whole idea of climbing up the tree, and then booby-trapping it to distract the guards, that was my contribution to the story.

Was there anything in-between the script and the story reel phase using zViz?
There was a lot of work already done on sets and character design, all of which I inherited. They just said, "Here it is!" I slightly changed the nature of what some of the weird creatures were. I made the ones that flew into vultures that would try to eat the bodies of the dead clone troopers. I guess you could say that was another script idea.

Did you have any involvement with the direction of the actors?
Yes, once we'd recorded and cut the temporary voices in, and then made any adjustments, we went down to Los Angeles and recorded the actual voices of the clones and Krell. So I was there for the final recording.

1 / Captain Rex's own adherence to protocol initially echoes that of his Jedi commander – a fact exploited by the corrupted Jedi.

2 / Filmmakers often arrange storyboard images from the production out in a physical grid so they can easily visualize the flow of events. Below, Walter Murch and Dave Filoni perform that very tactic.

2 /

3 /

3 / The episodes detailing the battle on Umbara explores the struggle of the clones as they face morally questionable orders from a corrupted general.

4 / Dave Filoni described the Umbaran technology as "PVC plastic", pointing out that the distinct anesthetic helped separate the Umbarans from the clones.

It's very important, I think, for the director to be there at the time of the recording.

The episode has a lot of action in it, but is also quite violent. There's a scene where some Umbarans walk past and the clones shoot them in the head.
That was another idea I had. And another was the amount of stomping that the scorpion tanks do. There are many clones that get killed by being stepped on. It's grisly, people being stepped on and so forth… I plead guilty to the grisly parts of the story, or emphasizing them in any way.

Is that because you think kids today can handle it?
I think so, but I wasn't thinking about the audience specifically. I thought it was my duty–I'd been invited to do this stuff and they were looking for somebody from the outside. So I guess I was pushing the envelope.

I think that's one of the very interesting things about the show. It gets into some pretty deep, philosophical waters about what an army is: Who are the soldiers in an army and what are they really doing? Do they obey orders without thinking or are they obliged to think on their feet and countermand an order if they know a better way to do it; and what's the cost of that?

It sounds like it intellectually engaged you.
Yes, it did. But all this is not specifically limited to my episode.

Did you get to see your episode before it went to air?
Yes, and I thought the picture was way too dark. When I saw the aired version of "The General," the darkness had been lightened. I don't know what knobs they twirled, but there was much more light, and yet it still looked like a dark planet. So I was much happier.

IN PURSUIT OF PERFECTION

Film director and editor Duwayne Dunham – best known to *Star Wars* fans for his visual effects editing work on *Return of the Jedi* (1983) – returned to the saga when he directed two episodes of *Star Wars: The Clone Wars*: Season Three's "Pursuit of Peace" and Season Four's "Water Wars".

How did you come to work on *The Clone Wars*?
George Lucas wanted to have guest directors from live-action come in to bring a different sensibility to the animation process. George was always saying, "Oh, give me that shot, but do this," and the guys who created the story reel animation sometimes didn't understand what was needed, so I would become almost an interpreter. I would try to learn how they're doing it, but do it as if it were live-action.

The first episode you directed, "Pursuit of Peace," featured more intrigue than action. Was it a tough episode to direct?

The way I look at things, everything's hard to direct. Sometimes you think, "Oh, I wish I just had a story with four people in one room. But when you get one of those, you think, I've got to have something else!"

Did you add any action to it?
Yeah, I did. There was a conversation in a dark alley and I said, "No, I don't want the conversation in a dark alley! Give me a bar or a nightclub!" So we did that nightclub scene with the dancers and saxophone players. Then I said, "These guys will go after Padmé, and there's a fight, and then they'll get on this speeder bike, and then the guy'll shoot his rocket-hand-thing and it'll blow the other off his feet!"

I worked with Dave Filoni to change it to bring it to life, and add entertainment. It's funny, because when I was doing that, I'd be doing these shots and quite often the guys would turn to me and say, "We've never done a shot like that!" I heard that when we changed it, George said, "This is the model for how we do this kind of story

1 /

in the future," because he wanted more episodes that were character driven, and not just endless action.

We used whatever assets we had. Each episode gets a few new assets, and that's Dave Filoni's territory. I was very happy with how it turned out. George was very happy. He never says too much, but I was a little nervous and excited to be in the editing room with George again. Sure enough, about two minutes into it, he's flying around with these new ideas!

Do you remember anything in particular that he changed?

The second episode I directed, "Water War," had a lot of changes! Dave and I worked to improve the main character, the kid (Lee Char, a Mon Calamari prince). It was also really interesting because (Mon Calamari leader) Ackbar hadn't been seen since *Jedi*. It was all underwater, so we were able to develop water cameras (virtual cameras that could be used to emulate the way things move underwater), so all the characters would be moving independent of one another in this liquid space. It was mostly about plotting out those battles.

I ran that episode for Dave early, and when he saw the first act he just went "Whoooooa!" He said, "Just do it. Keep going. This is good. Don't worry about how many assets you have in it."

I remember... George Lucas said, "Take that dorsal fin off Riff. He's a man, not a fish!" The very next thing I said was, "Can he still swim around, like this?" And George says, "Of course he can! He's a fish, not a man!" Dave and I just burst out laughing–that's just George's way!

What was it like filing animation compared to live action?

I keep telling the guys that I would love to come back! I just had so much fun... and it's exactly like live-action! We weren't using real people, but we were creating shots in exactly the same way. It's the same kind of rush when you break it down into individual shots and pieces, and then you cut it together. If it doesn't work, you can just go back and have the guys tweak the shot a little bit. It's really great!

1 / Riff Tamson was designed with flexible, fin-like feet, so that the character could realistically walk on land as well as move quickly in the ocean.

2 / The Mon Calamari swim into battle.

2 /

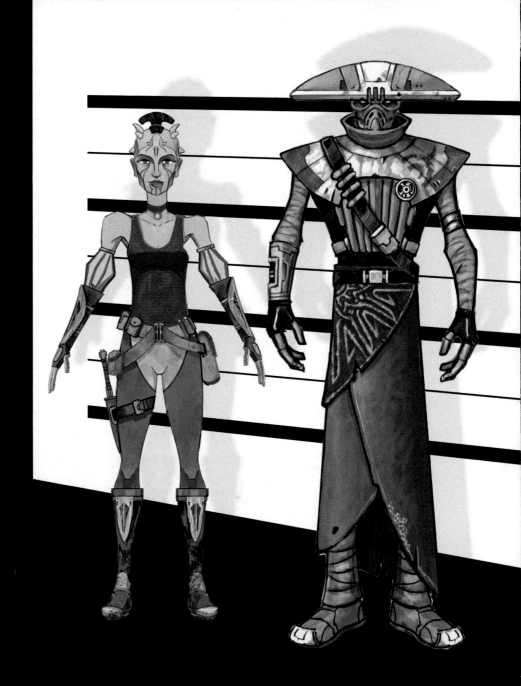

THE UNUSUAL SUSPECTS

Popular characters of *Star Wars* lore since their first appearance en masse in Star Wars: *The Empire Strikes Back*, the bounty hunters returned with a vengeance in Season 2 of *Star Wars: The Clone Wars*. Dave Filoni talks about the galactic tough guys!

BOUNTY BUNCH

"When it came to the bounty hunters, we really wanted them to have a lot of colorful elements to their costumes along with different little knives and bits of gear like all the details you see on Boba Fett's outfit. It's great that over the years the fans have decided, 'Oh, those are sonic wrenches,' and other details," says Dave Filoni. "It might have just been a piece of metal that was shoved in the pocket for effect! We try to make our bounty hunters interesting like that. They definitely have more logos; for some reason there always seems to be a slight NASCAR-effect to the bounty hunters when you see all these emblems. I think that comes from Boba Fett being yellow-shouldered with green armor, and then later having red gauntlets. It makes them stand out. You know instantly they're not Republic or Separatists.

"It's fun to pay off that season-opening promise of 'Rise of the Bounty Hunters', because here come a whole bunch of them!"

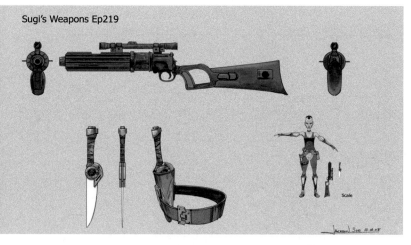

Sugi's Weapons Ep219

Scale

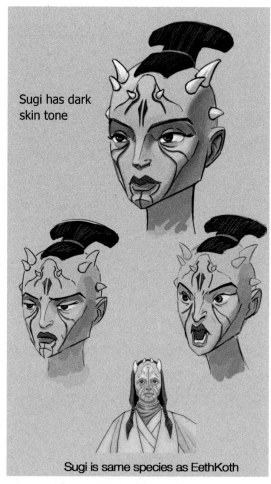

Sugi has dark skin tone

Sugi is same species as EethKoth

SUGI All Sugi/Sugi weapon illustrations by Jackson Sze.

"She is a Zabrak [the same species as Darth Maul]. We mainly used Eeth Koth as an inspiration for her. There was some debate on whether or not she should have horns. We wondered, do female Zabraks have horns? But let's face it, she's a lot cooler if she has horns than if she doesn't! So since it was never defined, we decided to give her horns.

We had a certain way we wanted her shoulders to puff out with a kind of red striping, so there's a little bit of a pirate element to her, with a very specific hairstyle. She really lends herself to being a visually exciting character, but still very human-looking. She turned out to be someone with a really fun attitude. I love the scenes where she's talking with Obi-Wan Kenobi. She seems to stand toe-to-toe with him really well as another very independent, well-spoken being… and she's great with a blaster!"

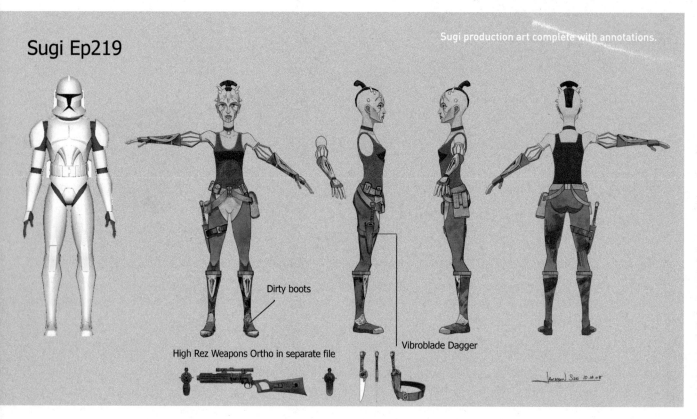

Sugi Ep219

Sugi production art complete with annotations.

Dirty boots

High Rez Weapons Ortho in separate file

Vibroblade Dagger

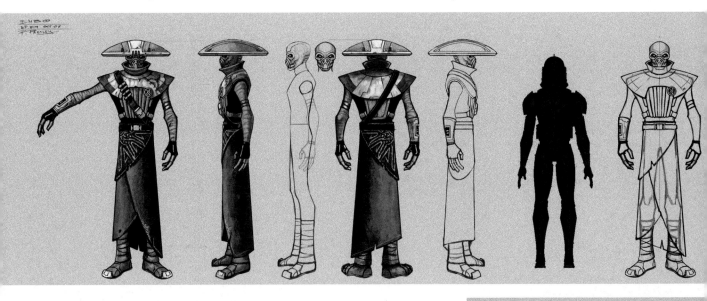

EMBO

All Embo and Embo weapon illustrations by Pat Presley.

"Embo was a design handed to us by George Lucas from earlier concept work. We just modified him a bit. He became a favorite character with the team at Lucasfilm Animation. I don't know what it is, maybe it's that hat, but something about him just connected. Steward Lee [the director], and I really wanted to expand what Embo did, as far as action, to show how skilled these bounty hunters are with their weaponry. Design-wise, there wasn't a lot to develop, because we had such a good head-start from George, but we decided that we wouldn't let him speak English. We just went full-out with an alien tongue that we invented. We don't often do full alien speaking characters in *The Clone Wars*, mainly because of the amount of subtitling that would require— and that's a disappointment. But here we had characters reacting to what Embo says, like they do to R2-D2."

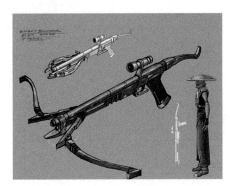

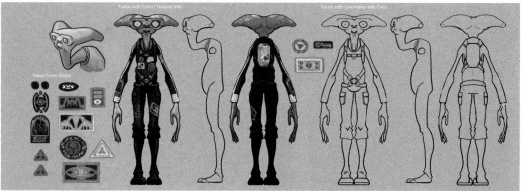

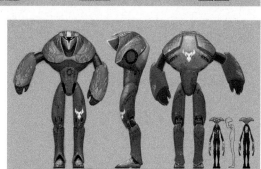

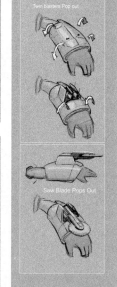

SERIPAS

"This was another design that came to us from George. He is basically a big suit of armor and George wanted this little guy inside him. Wayne Lo [the design artist] did this breakdown for him, which is the exploded view drawing of Seripas that just looks like a Japanese toy. I loved the way it would open up. We wanted to have a lot of little colored lights and stuff inside so we could really see these lights on his face when he's inside the big suit of armor.

"He turned out very cool, but he had a much more expanded role at one point that we had to cut down for time. We have these cool bounty hunters and some of them don't get to do a lot. Once I saw him without the armor on, I wanted him to have a lot of patches on his flight suit. And one of the patches I asked Wayne to include is the *Star Wars* fanclub patch of Darth Vader. So if you look closely, you'll see this little patch that looks a little bit like a Vader helmet. It's that one that he's wearing on his uniform!"

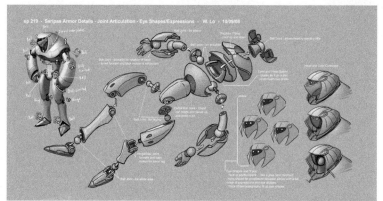

All Seripas images by Wayne Lo

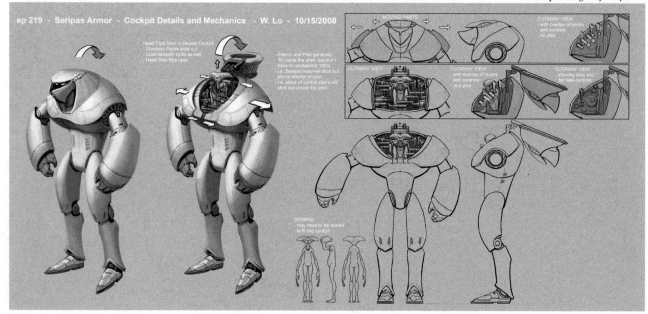

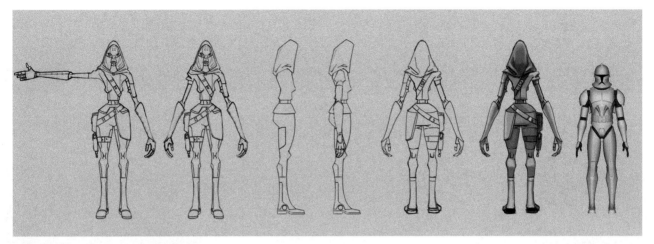

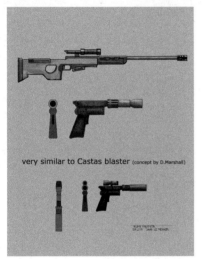

very similar to Castas blaster (concept by D.Marshall)

RUMI PARAMITA

George will often send us a design and say, 'I want it to look something like this.' Then we have to take it and bring it into *The Clone Wars* world, and sometimes it changes a lot and sometimes it doesn't. But we had a great start with Rumi. She started as a very small mouse, very narrow, which guided how we were going to have the voice-acting done. She's just a very bizarre, classic type of alien, with a large head and thin limbs.

All Rumi and Rumi weapon images by David Le Merrer

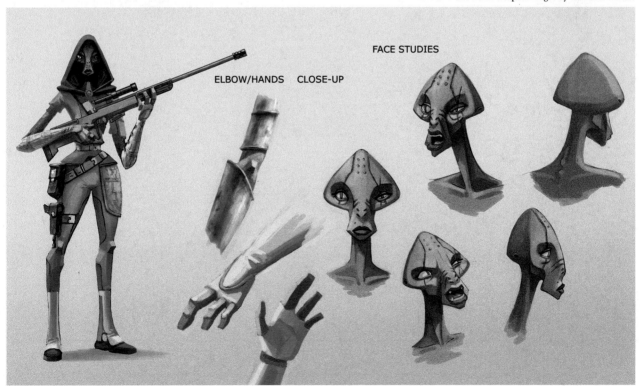

ELBOW/HANDS CLOSE-UP

FACE STUDIES

BRING HOME THE GALAXY... FROM FAR, FAR AWAY!